D0194385

PRO-SUMER POWER!

BILL QUAIN, PH.D.

PRO-SUMER POWER!

*How to Create Wealth by
Buying Smarter,
Not Cheaper!*

INTI

PUBLISHING & RESOURCE BOOKS

Pro-sumer Power!
How to Create Wealth by Buying Smarter, Not Cheaper
By Bill Quain, Ph.D.

Printed in the United States of America
First edition April 2000

ISBN: 1-891279-04-1
Published by INTI Publishing & Resource Books, Inc.
intipublishing.com
Tampa, FL

Cover design by Winters Design
Layout by Bayou Graphics

To my wife, Jeanne, and my two daughters, Amanda and Kathleen. In case you're wondering why I asked you to be in the photo on the back cover, here is my answer:

"What I do, I do for us."

Love, Dad

FROM THE DESK OF BILL QUAIN, PH.D.

If You Want to Have More, You Have to Think Like a Store!

Fortune magazine calls the New Millennium the "Age of the Consumer." And for good reason. With the advent of on-line shopping and the expansion of huge discount chains, prices for goods and services continue to drop, "saving" consumers billions of dollars every year.

But wait — are consumers really "saving" when they buy at discount? Or are they spending themselves into the poorhouse while the giant e-tailers and retailers are racking up record profits?

When you buy a $100 item at 40% discount, you don't "save" $40. *You spend $60!* When you take $60 from your net worth to buy a consumable, you not only lose the $60, you lose the ability to invest that $60 and grow more money over time. That's why consuming is such a drain on your net worth — consuming takes away from, rather than adds to, your bottom line.

Truth is, the vast majority of *consumers* will never build financial security because they've been conditioned by advertising to buy products and services that lose value over time. *Consumer-thinking spends money*, which leads to diminished assets and diminished dreams.

The huge stores that sell consumers discounted products, on the other hand, are *producers* of wealth, racking up record profits for themselves and their shareholders. *Producer-thinking invests money* with the idea of making money and building equity, which are the keys to wealth creation.

Today, thanks to a paradigm-shattering concept called *pro-sumer thinking*, average people can enjoy the best of both worlds — *they can produce wealth while they consume!* That's why I say that *pro-sumer thinking* is "buying smarter, not cheaper."

Pro-sumers have more because they think like the store. If you owned a Wal-Mart, you wouldn't buy from K-Mart, would you? In effect, pro-sumers own their own "store" — My-Mart, I call it. Pro-sumers learn to buy from My-Mart and then teach others to do the same, which enables them to create wealth while they spend. Pro-sumers are in businesss *for* themselves... but not *by* themselves.

It's a simple concept that is revolutionizing the way people buy and work. When you change your thinking and buying habits from short-term consumer thinking to long-term pro-sumer thinking, you can change your life.

Don't discount your dreams!

Bill Quain

Bill Quain, Ph.D.

ALSO BY BILL QUAIN, PH.D.

- *Reclaiming the American Dream*

- *10 Rules to Break & 10 Rules to Make*

ACKNOWLEDGMENT

Like most of my books, this one was two years in the making. During that time, the manuscript underwent many changes. Being human, I resisted some of the changes at first, but in the end, they greatly improved the final book.

I owe a great deal of thanks to some special people whose support, creativity, patience, and attention to detail were instrumental in bringing this book from concept to completion.

First of all, I'd like to thank the editorial staff at INTI Publishing for their tremendous contributions to the final product. Many thanks to Steve Price for his tireless work on the book. Early on Steve saw the vision for the book, added some terrific insights, and helped shape the book into its present form. A big "thank you" goes to Katherine Glover and Burke Hedges for keeping Steve and me on track. Our many marathon editing sessions brought out the best in all of us and greatly improved the final manuscript.

As always, special thanks to my wife, Jeanne, and to my mother, Kay Quain, for their ongoing contributions, both large and small.

Last but not least, a resounding "thank you" to my invaluable assistant, Janet Soto, for stepping in and handling dozens of tasks that would have otherwise kept me from completing this book.

To all of you I extend my sincerest gratitude. I couldn't have done it without you!

CONTENTS

INTRODUCTION

A MODERN-DAY PARABLE: PRO-SUMERS VS. DEEP DISCOUNTERS

The common misperception is that you have to work harder to earn more. Ultimately, your earnings will increase when you change your thinking — rather than your activities.

— Brian Koslow
author, *365 Ways to Become a Millionaire*

I'd like to open by telling you a story about Stan, a shopkeeper in a small Midwestern town who outsmarted a couple of big discount stores that were threatening to force him out of business. The story goes like this:

Stan owned and operated Stan's Store, a general store that was the centerpiece of Main Street. Stan made a nice living for himself and his family. And by all accounts, he deserved it, for he was loved and respected throughout the town.

One day Stan heard sawing and hammering on both sides of his store. Within months two new discount stores opened up, one on either side of him. The two new discount stores had wide aisles and colorful displays, and they sold the same merchandise as Stan's general store — *but at lower prices!*

On opening day the store to the left of Stan's Store featured a humongous neon sign above the front door:

GIANT CHAIN
DISCOUNT STORE
Rock Bottom Prices!

The next day the store to the right of Stan's Store responded with a huge flashing sign above its door:

BUY-IN-BULK
SUPER DISCOUNT STORE
Lowest Prices In Town!

It didn't take long for word to spread that prices were cheaper in the new discount stores. Before long Stan's business dwindled to nothing. He watched helplessly as his long-time customers and friends passed by his doors shopping for bargains. He waved as they entered first one discount store... then the other... comparing prices to "save" $1 on a box of detergent or $10 on a new VCR.

Stan knew he had to make some drastic changes fast or he was doomed. The obvious solution was to cut prices and compete with the stores on either side of him. But that was financial suicide. Stan's single store could never buy products as cheaply as a discount chain with a thousand stores.

"There must be another way!" Stan thought to himself.

The Birth of the Pro-sumer Revolution

Then one day a former customer entered Stan's Store, glanced around and blurted, *"Oops, this isn't the store I was looking for. This is Stan's Store."* The former customer turned on his heels and headed back out the door.

"This is Stan's Store! This is Stan's Store!" The words kept ringing in the shopkeeper's head.

"People think of this store as belonging to me," Stan thought to himself. "Customers don't think of this store as THEIR store. They think of it as MY store. What if I started thinking of my customers as business affiliates instead of consumers? What if my new business affiliates could earn money and build equity while shopping here? My guess is they'd stop buying from someone else and start buying from themselves."

It was a revolutionary concept, but Stan understood that desperate times called for desperate measures. He gathered his employees and asked them to help him redesign his business so that customers would start thinking and acting like joint-venture partners. The employees loved the idea and started coming up with great ideas for a revolutionary new business model.

"Let's start encouraging our customers to become affiliates by helping them set up their own referral-based businesses," suggested one employee.

"The more products our affiliates buy, the deeper the discounts they should receive," suggested another.

"How about offering rebates on all purchases?" asked another.

"Affiliates who refer friends and family to our store could earn commissions on their purchases," suggested another.

"We spend a huge amount of money on advertising," commented a long-time employee. *"What if we stopped running expensive ads and commercials and started using the most powerful form of advertising — referral marketing — one satisfied cus-*

tomer to another? Then we could use the money we saved on advertising to pay our new affiliates for directing traffic to our store."

Within a week, Stan had totally restructured Stan's Store. It was no longer just HIS store. Stan still warehoused the merchandise, but the store shared a portion of its revenues with its new business affiliates, each of whom owned and operated his own home-based business. Stan and his employees cheered as the old Stan's Store sign was taken down and replaced with a brand new sign. It said:

YOUR STORE
Where It Pays to Buy from Yourself

Happy Ending to Stan's Story

Stan's daring new business model turned out to be far more successful than he ever dreamed! Most people loved the affiliate concept behind Your Store, and within months the business exploded.

Twenty-five years after the "Your Store" sign went up, the company had evolved from one small retail store in the Midwest to hundreds of mega-distribution centers throughout the world.

During those 25 years, hundreds of thousands of Stan's referral-based business affiliates discovered they could supplement their income several hundred dollars a month by referring their acquaintances to Your Store. Thousands of Your Store's most ambitious affiliates were able to "retire" from their traditional jobs and earn a substantial income by building their own referral-based businesses. And hundreds of the hardest-working affiliates became millionaires by building huge organizations of Your Store consumers and affiliates.

Oh, sure, some people told Stan that his new business model would never work. It was too "radical." Too different. But Stan pursued *his dream* of helping others make money so they could pursue *their dreams*. Fortunately for thousands of successful Your Store affiliates, Stan's dream won out over the nay sayers, and in less than 25 years, Your Store evolved into a multi-billion dollar Fortune 500 company.

Today Stan is retired and living in Florida. His four children operate Your Store International, Inc., a Fortune 500 company with several million affiliates throughout the world. As for the future, it looks brighter than ever, for Stan's children are taking the company to a whole new level with YourStore.com, a virtual on-line mall where it still pays self-employed affiliates to buy smarter, not cheaper.

Launching the Pro-sumer Revolution

The parable of Stan vs. the deep discounters points out a powerful lesson for every person who has ever told themselves they "saved" money by buying something at discount.

The truth is, you can't literally "save" money when you buy at deep discount. Yes, you spend less when you buy at discount. But you're still spending. And spending *subtracts from your bank account*.

THERE MUST BE ANOTHER WAY!

Fortunately, there is another way. I call it "pro-suming." And it's a proven way whereby *you can produce and consume at the same time!* No, that wasn't a misprint. Just to make sure your eyes aren't playing tricks on you, I'll write that statement in all capital letters:

THERE IS A WAY YOU CAN PRODUCE AND CONSUME AT THE SAME TIME!

In other words, people who buy smarter, not cheaper — and then teach others to do the same — *can literally make money while they spend money.*

When you change your thinking from consumer thinking to pro-sumer thinking, amazing things begin to happen — you start to *add to* your bank account, rather than *subtract from* it.

That's why I say, "If you want to have more, you have to think like the store." Stores are in business to produce wealth, not to consume wealth. Once you grasp the power of this concept, you'll be on your way to creating more wealth for you and your family.

Pro-sumer thinking changed Stan's bank account... and his life.

It can do the same for you.

PART ONE

THE PRO-SUMER MENTALITY

When you buy at discount, you subtract from your bank account. When you pro-sume, you add to your bank account.

Buying a home is a classic example of how smart pro-sumers can spend money and make money at the same time.

1

WHY YOU SHOULD ENLIST IN THE PRO-SUMER REVOLUTION

Benjamin Franklin may have discovered electricity — but it was the man who invented the meter who made money.

> — Earl Wilson
> Syndicated newspaper columnist

The word *pro-sumer* is a combination of the words *producer* and *consumer*. Producers make money. Consumers spend money. Pro-sumers make money while they spend.

Pro-suming is a proven concept that's been around for years, and a growing legion of people who understand this concept and are teaching it to others are making fortunes.

If You Own Your Home, You're a Pro-Sumer

A classic example of pro-suming is owning your own home. When you buy a home, you're buying a product, like a car or a couch. Unlike cars and couches, however, well-maintained homes in good neighborhoods gain in value over the years. In other words, a home appreciates instead of depreciates over time. In addition, homeowners build equity in their homes with each monthly mortgage payment they make.

The combination of appreciation coupled with the equity in a home (not to mention the fact that homeowners can write off the mortgage interest on their yearly income taxes) adds to the homeowner's net worth. That's why homes are far and away the single biggest source of wealth for the vast majority of North Americans. Government statistics show that 67% of the average American's net worth is tied up in their home, proving that owning your own home is a terrific investment!

Home ownership is the classic example of the power of pro-suming!

When you buy a home, you're making money while you're spending money. In the long run, you're creating more wealth for yourself and your family. That's why owning a home is referred to as an investment instead of an expense.

The money we spend buying the home increases, rather than decreases, our net worth. What a concept — and what a great deal for everyone involved! The homeowners create more wealth each time they make their monthly mortgage payment. And the mortgage companies create wealth by earning interest on the loan. As I said, home ownership is a classic example of pro-suming — homeowners produce wealth as they consume. It's a win/win for everyone!

Pro-Suming Every Time You Buy

The best news of all is that pro-suming isn't limited to home ownership. The same pro-suming principles that work to create wealth for homeowners — *equity, appreciation, and tax advantages* — can be applied to create wealth for you and your family virtually every time you buy a product or service. The key is to think LONG TERM like a homeowner, instead of thinking SHORT TERM like a renter. In the long run, it's better to pay an extra $100 a month for a mortgage and build equity than to "save" $100 a month renting and build nothing in return. *In brief, the keys to pro-suming are to buy smarter, not cheaper... to think long term, not short term... and to think like an owner, not a customer.*

Virtually anyone who understands the basic principles behind pro-suming can learn to create wealth by changing their daily buying habits. You don't have to earn a Ph.D. in economics to understand these principles. They're so simple and basic that even elementary-age kids running the neighborhood lemonade stand can learn them in a few minutes.

I'm always amazed when I run into people who refuse to acknowledge the power of pro-suming. Most of these people own their own homes, and they'd never be caught dead renting.

"Why throw your money away on rent when you can own," they'll say. Yet these same people will fold their arms and close their minds when I talk about extending the concept of home ownership to all of their buying. Go figure.

It reminds me of Oscar Wilde's great line, "Don't confuse me with the facts!" The fact is pro-suming, like owning your own home, just makes good sense. And if some close-minded people can't accept that, then it's their loss, not mine. Next.

Pro-suming: How the Rich Get Richer

Rich people have always understood the power of pro-suming. In the best-selling book *The Millionaire Next Door*, the authors list the key strategies most millionaires use to accumulate their wealth. Amazingly, these strategies are so simple and powerful that anyone can dramatically increase their wealth by putting them into practice.

According to *The Millionaire Next Door*, millionaires understand the difference between *investing* (money *grows*) and *spending* (money *goes*). Millionaires purchase *assets* that increase in value, such as quality stocks, instead of *liabilities* that lose their value over time, such as expensive furniture. *Millionaires own their own businesses* or are *equity partners* in the companies they work for. Millionaires own their own homes. Millionaires delay short-term gratification for long-term financial security. In short, millionaires look for opportunities to make money when they spend money.

In a word, *millionaires are pro-sumers!*

The Road to Financial Freedom Allows U-Turns

Billionaire J. Paul Getty once observed that "If you want to get rich, just find someone making lots of money and do what he's doing." Well, rich people are pro-sumers. They have more because they think like the store — they think like the owner rather than the customer and then act accordingly. So if you want what *millionaires have*, you have to do what *millionaires do*. And millionaires pro-sume rather than consume. It's that simple.

What about you? Are you a "millionaire next door"? Or are you working harder just to stay even? If you're working harder, you're not alone. According to a United Nations study, Americans work more hours today than any other industrialized country — including the work-obsessed Japanese!

Unfortunately, working longer hours doesn't necessarily equate to creating more wealth. A recent *USA Today* survey reported that half of Americans have less than $2,500 in savings, and when workers were asked how long it would take to fall behind in bill payments if they lost their jobs, 54% replied "three months or less."

The good news is that it's never too late for people to adopt strategies that can turn their lives around. It's like *The Family Circus* cartoon by Bill Keane titled "Grandma's Advice." Grandma is surrounded by her four little grandchildren who are hanging on her every word. Her advice is timeless: "If you're ever headed the wrong way in life, remember the road to Heaven allows U-turns."

Grandma's advice is right on the mark — it's never too late to change our behavior. Her sage advice applies to finances just as surely as it applies to salvation: *The road to financial freedom allows U-turns.*

What Direction Are You Headed In?

If you've been heading in the wrong financial direction because you've been thinking and acting like a consumer instead of a pro-sumer, it's not too late to make a U-turn.

If you're headed in the wrong direction on the financial road to freedom, most likely it's because you didn't know any better! *You were just following the crowd!* Like most people, you bought into the wrong plan — the consumer plan. And the only ones getting rich from the consumer plan are the stores.

That's why I say if you want to have more, you have to think like a store. Hey, there's no law that says only stores can sell products and create wealth. If they can do it, you can do it, too! All it takes is an understanding of how pro-suming works.

The first step to making your U-turn from a consumer to a pro-sumer is to open your mind to some new concepts. As a wise person once said, "Your mind is like a parachute. It only works when it's open."

You have to open your mind so that you can replace your old consumer thinking with new pro-sumer thinking. When you do that, you'll start heading in a different financial direction — the same direction the millionaires next door are headed in.

It may not be the most popular direction.

But it's the direction I want to go in.

What about you?

2

CHANGE YOUR THINKING AND YOU CHANGE YOUR LIFE

To think is to act.
— Ralph Waldo Emerson

I n the mid-1990s, Apple Computer was on the brink of bankruptcy. Steven Jobs revitalized the company in the late '90s by introducing a breakthrough computer he called the "iMac."

The ad campaign for the iMac was as creative and provocative as the computer itself. The ads featured black and white photographs of the century's greatest thinkers and innovators, such as Albert Einstein, Mohandas Gandhi, and Amelia Earhart, to name a few. This simple slogan anchored each photo:

THINK DIFFERENT.

Why 'Think Different'?

"THINK DIFFERENT." That hasn't always been great advice. In Galileo's time, thinking different could have gotten you burned at the stake.

But today it's imperative that people learn to challenge conventional wisdom and think different. Relying on conventional wisdom won't get you anything but *conventional* results. (Given the fact that almost half of the *conventional* workers with *conventional* jobs earn less than $25,000 a year and carry $2,000 or more in monthly credit card debt, well, who needs that kind of *conventional result!*)

Great thinkers are different thinkers. They don't fall into the trap of thinking and acting like the herd. They're mavericks. They break away from the herd mentality. It's the mavericks who blaze new trails and open new frontiers. Henry Ford was a maverick. The late Sam Walton, founder of Wal-Mart, was a maverick. Jeff Bezos, the founder of Amazon.com, and a dozen other Internet billionaires are mavericks.

It pays, literally, to THINK DIFFERENT.

Jobs and Discounts: THINKING THE SAME

What about the vast majority of people... those people who THINK THE SAME... instead of THINK DIFFERENT? How do they go about producing wealth?

Most people who THINK THE SAME about producing wealth get a job. That's the obvious way to produce wealth, isn't it? When people with jobs want to produce more wealth, they seek a promotion. Or they look for a better-paying job. Or they work overtime. Or they get a second or even third job.

They may change their jobs, but they don't change their thinking. They THINK THE SAME. That's why today, Americans work longer hours than any other nation.

Most people THINK THE SAME when it comes to shopping, too. We've been taught to "save" money by buying stuff at discount or on sale. Shopping at discount stores has become a national obsession as more and more shoppers seek to "save" by buying cheaper, not smarter. Witness the dramatic growth of huge discount superstores such as Wal-Mart... K-Mart... The Home Depot... Costco... and the like.

Consumers are lining up at discount stores and surfing the latest discount website trying to "save" money by buying things cheaper. But they're only kidding themselves. You can't "save" money by consuming, no matter what price you pay, because the money is going out, not coming in.

You Can't 'Save' By Buying at Discount

People who THINK THE SAME and try to produce wealth in a job or "save" money by buying stuff at discount are like the guy who lost his car keys late one night. The man paced frantically back and forth under a bright street lamp searching for his keys.

Several strangers stopped to help. Before long there were 10 people combing every inch under the street light. Still no keys.

"Are you sure you dropped them under the street light?" one of the strangers asked.

"No," replied the man, *"I actually dropped them in that dark alley behind us. But I decided to look under this street lamp because the light is so much better."*

People are the same way — they search to produce more wealth where they can see better, that is, in the same old familiar places — in their jobs and by "saving" money buying at discount.

HELLO-O-O! If you're looking to produce significantly more wealth by working harder at your job or by buying products and services at discount, you're looking in the wrong place! Nothing wrong with jobs, you understand. I love my job as a college professor. But I don't count solely on my job to make me financially free!

Likewise, I don't count on "saving" money by buying at discount. Truth is, deep discounts weren't designed to create wealth for consumers by "saving" them money. Deep discounts were designed to *create wealth for store owners by taking money from consumers*.

Now, don't get me wrong — I'm not saying you should always pay full retail prices when you could buy the same thing at a discount. That would be silly. Discounts are great for consumers, there's no question about that. And everybody, even billionaires, loves a bargain.

But don't kid yourself that you're "saving" money when you buy at a discount. When you consume products, you're *subtracting from* your bank account, not *adding to* your bank account. You're spending, not saving.

As I've said before, buying cheaper isn't designed to create income. People who try to focus on building more assets by buying cheaper are looking under the street lamp because the light is better, not because it's the best place to look. *They're focusing their attention and basing their actions on the wrong set of assumptions*. They're focusing their attention on the wrong thing — they're focusing on "outgo" rather than income.

The Danger of Focusing on the Wrong Thing

It's easier to focus on the wrong thing than you might think. It happens to us all the time. Here's a little test to see if you're *focusing on the right thing*:

Instructions: *Using a pencil, draw the quickest path
from the start of the maze to the finish.
Time yourself to see how long it takes.*

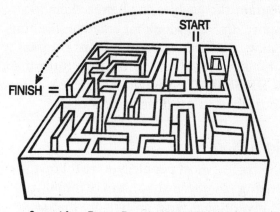

Concept from *Escape From the Maze,* by James Higgins

Are you done? How long did it take you to solve this
problem? If you were like most people, it took you 30 seconds to two minutes to draw a line through the twisting
maze.

Would you be surprised to learn that *some people can solve
this same puzzle in less than a second*? How? They draw a
curved line around the maze or they draw a straight line
through the maze from start to finish.

"That's against the rules!" you may shout.

But look at the directions again. Nothing says you have
to stay within the lines... or even within the maze itself.
But most people draw a twisting line through the maze
because they fall victim to conventional thinking. They've
drawn lines through mazes before, so they *assume* they
should draw a twisting line through this one. As a result,
conventional thinkers spend a lot of extra time and effort
solving the puzzle because *they're focusing on the wrong thing*
— they're focusing on the twists and turns in the maze,
not the directions.

If you fell into the trap of conventional thinking, you, too, *focused on the wrong thing* and missed the shortest route from start to finish. Unconventional thinkers, on the other hand, program themselves to change their focus. They look for shortcuts. They look for creative solutions. They seek out new... and better... and unconventional ways of solving problems. In other words, they force themselves to THINK DIFFERENT! And when we think different, we position ourselves to get different results.

Think Like a Store

Folks, if you're like most people, you're following conventional thinking when you shop. You're thinking like a consumer. Conventional wisdom tells us that *stores produce wealth by selling stuff.* Conventional wisdom tells us that *we consume our wealth by buying stuff* from stores. Conventional wisdom tells us that stores get richer. We get poorer. And that's just the way things are.

Hold it right there! Take off your conventional wisdom glasses and look at the directions again! Where is it written that you have to think and act like a consumer? Where is it written that you have to work your way through the store maze, buying as you go? (By the way, ever notice how the aisles in supermarkets are set up like mazes? Coincidence? Think about it....)

"THINK DIFFERENT!" I say.

You can crash through the store maze. Or you can go around the store maze. You can stop thinking like a consumer and start thinking like a producer. You can start thinking like an owner of the business, instead of thinking like an employee. You can think like the store and position yourself to produce wealth, just as easily as you can think like a customer and consume wealth. In other words, you can start thinking like a pro-sumer, instead of thinking like a consumer.

The first step to THINKING DIFFERENT is to *take off your consumer's hat... and put on a producer's hat instead.* That simple shift in thinking is what separates the haves from the have nots. The rich from the poor. The wishful thinkers from the "goal getters." That's why I say, *"If you want to have more, you have to think like the store."*

Are You a Rich Dad?... Or a Poor Dad?

Rich Dad, Poor Dad is a wonderful book that clearly illustrates what I'm getting at. The author, Robert Kiyosaki, grew up with "two dads." His biological father was his "poor dad," an educated professional who taught his son that conventional thinking was the way to wealth: "Go to college... work hard... earn money... and climb the corporate ladder" was the poor dad's advice.

Kiyosaki's "rich dad" was the father of a friend who encouraged his own son and Kiyosaki not to work for money, but to let money work for them! The philosophy of the rich dad was surprisingly simple: The key to getting rich is to understand the difference between a liability and an asset.

"An asset puts money in your pocket," the rich dad taught them. "A liability takes money out. Rich people acquire assets. The poor and middle class acquire liabilities, *but they think they are assets.*"

In other words, most people might *think* they're "saving" money when they buy at discount, but all they're really doing is acquiring another liability. THINK DIFFERENT!

What Do You See When You Shop?

There's an old Spanish expression that sums up how our thinking affects our outlook on life: *"When a pickpocket meets a priest, all he sees are pockets."*

Isn't that a great expression? It illustrates how our thoughts color the way we see the world. Pickpockets think of only one thing — stealing valuables out of people's pockets. Before pickpockets can change their behavior, they have to change their thinking. What do you think would happen if the pickpocket would "think different" and view the world from the priest's point of view? His life would take a 180-degree turn, wouldn't it?

The same phenomenon applies to consumers — they see the world as a place to *spend money* rather than produce money. When consumers visit a deep discount store or website, all they see are products to spend money on. But what happens when consumers look at those products from the store's point of view? They begin to see assets, instead of liabilities. And they begin making the transition from poor dads (and moms)... to rich dads (and moms).

If you keep thinking like a consumer, looking to "save" money by buying everything at discount, then the only thing you'll end up discounting is your dreams! When you focus on buying at discount, you end up with a garage full of stuff you bought for 40% off. Two years later, when you decide to get rid of all the clutter, you're lucky to get a penny on the dollar at a garage sale. You may have "saved" 40% in the short run, but *in the long run you've discounted your dreams 100% because you can't afford them anymore!*

Folks, it's time for YOU to think different, too! It's time to think like the store... *so that YOU can have more!*

PART TWO

PRO-SUMING IN THE NEW MILLENNIUM

The Internet makes it easier than ever for consumers to spend money.

That's why it's imperative that people start thinking like producers, instead of consumers.

By buying on-line from themselves, pro-sumers can leverage the power of the Internet to create more income, instead of "out-go."

3

THE INTERNET IS THE KING KONG OF COMMERCE — AND IT'S STILL ONLY A BABY!

In five years, every company will be an Internet company — or they won't be companies at all.

> — Andy Grove
> Chairman, Intel

Did you ever happen to catch one of those old black and white monster movies from the early 1950s on late-night TV? — movies like *The Tarantula... Colossal Man...* and *Godzilla*?

The monsters would change with each movie, but the plot was basically the same: An atomic bomb would explode somewhere on Earth, sending a mushroom cloud of radioactivity into the air. When the cloud descended, the radioactivity would cause everything in its path to mutate and grow to 1,000 times its normal size

The Internet: Stranger Than Fiction

Those old "science fiction" movies from the '50s were entertaining, but, in truth, they were more fiction than science. Today, only 50 years later, we live in a world that's just the opposite — *science is stranger than fiction!*

No, we don't have radioactive clouds and mutated monsters threatening the world. But we do have an electronic "e-cloud" enveloping the world, mutating millions of computers into a single, living organism that is rapidly encircling the globe.

We call this hi-tech "monster" the Internet.

The Internet monster is already huge — and it's only a baby! Consider this: Right now 300 million of the world's six billion people are hooked up on the Internet — that's almost one out of every 20 people. Experts predict that by 2010, *one billion people will have access to the Internet!* One billion people all across the globe, separated by distance but connected via an electronic superhighway — one billion people who are just a point and click away from communicating with... buying from... and selling to each other. Science fiction, indeed!

What's All the Fuss About?

A few years ago when I was just getting going on the Internet, a friend of mine described it as "a technology looking for a purpose." At the time I thought he was right. I don't feel that way anymore. Today I feel about the Internet the same way business people feel about the fax machine — *"How did I ever get along without it?"* If the Internet were nothing more than a way to send e-mail, it would rank as one of the greatest inventions in history. But it's so much more!

The Internet is a library. A phone book. A daily newspaper. A video arcade. A travel agent. A museum. A bank. A stockbroker. An art gallery. An encyclopedia. A virtual office. A photo album. A music store. A video store. A meeting room. A political action committee. A post office. A mail room. A car dealership. A bookstore. A giant mall. Well, you get the idea.

Any one of these functions would justify its existence. But it's all of these things at the same time — AND MORE! Already the Internet is dramatically changing the way we live and work.

The Age of the Consumer

The most talked about function on the Internet is e-commerce, that is, buying and selling products and services via the Internet. *Fortune* magazine calls e-commerce the greatest boon to consumers since the introduction of the department store at the turn of the 20th century. *Fortune* goes on to say that, thanks to the Internet, the New Millennium will be the "Age of the Consumer."

E-commerce is already big, BIG business, and it's only a baby. One financial writer compares the evolution of the Internet to a baseball game. At this point, the Internet is just starting to take pre-game batting practice. *The 9-inning game hasn't even started yet!*

Forecasts indicate that e-commerce is making money hand over fist, but that THE BIG MONEY HASN'T BEEN MADE YET, as indicated by the graph.

Why is e-com-

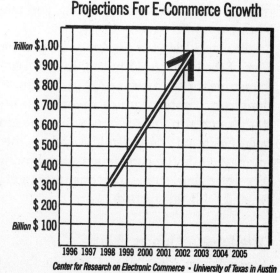

Projections For E-Commerce Growth

Trillion $1.00
$ 900
$ 800
$ 700
$ 600
$ 500
$ 400
$ 300
$ 200
Billion $ 100

1996 1997 1998 1999 2000 2001 2002 2003 2004 2005

Center for Research on Electronic Commerce · University of Texas in Austin

27

merce such a boon for consumers? Two reasons: Convenience and lower prices. Let's take a moment to discuss each of these.

Shopping is certainly convenient on the Internet, no argument there. No crowded stores. No traffic jams. No long checkout lanes. Stores are open 24 hours a day, 7 days a week, 365 days a year. And your order is delivered to your door. It doesn't get any more convenient than that.

As for lower prices — well, consumers are definitely in the Internet's driver's seat! Here's why: By its very nature, the Internet is fast, vast, and efficient. It's a whole lot cheaper to open and operate a "clicks and mortar" cyber store than it is to build and operate a "bricks and mortar" traditional store. Plus e-commerce sites eliminate the middlemen. Those savings get passed on to consumers. The result is the Age of the Consumer — *or so it would seem!*

Age of the Consumer?... Or Age of the Producer?

Put on your thinking cap for a moment. At the end of the day, what are all of these e-commerce sites in business for? To make a profit, correct? At first glance it may seem like they're doing you a favor selling you merchandise at discount.

But what looks like the Age of the Consumer is actually the Age of the Producer! You see, in the Age of the Producer, consumers pay lower prices in the short run. But in the long run, it's the producers who come out ahead because they're creating *more assets* while consumers are *creating more liabilities!* It's an endless cycle — the producers make money while the consumers spend money. The producers get richer while the consumers get poorer. What's wrong with this picture?

The Casino Always Wins!

Steve Wynn, the CEO of Mirage Resorts in Las Vegas,

knows a thing or two about producers and consumers. Wynn has worked in the gambling industry for more than 25 years, and during that time his casinos have produced billions of dollars of profits for owners and investors.

When a reporter asked Wynn which game of chance offered the best odds in a casino, Wynn smiled and replied, "*If you want to make money in a casino, own one.*" Why? Because the odds are stacked in favor of the house. As a result, the casino will always produce wealth while the gamblers will always consume wealth.

Wynn's sage advice applies not just to people who gamble but to every consumer. *If you want to make money in a store, own one!* People tell themselves they can "save" money when they buy stuff on sale or at discounts, just like gamblers tell themselves they can make money playing poker or throwing dice. But in the end, they're just kidding themselves.

It doesn't matter whether consumers buy on sale or online... whether they buy at cost or below cost... they'll never be able to spend their way to wealth. NEVER! Consumers are just making producers richer! By definition, consuming means money goes out, instead of coming in. If you think casinos have the odds in their favor, what about stores? They ALWAYS win!

Do You Want to Be the Gorilla or the Banana?

Not long ago I was reading an investment newsletter that referred to producers as "gorillas" and consumers as "bananas." The analogy paints a vivid picture, doesn't it? Now I ask you, what would you rather be — the gorilla or the banana? — the person MAKING the money?... or the person SPENDING the money?

The simple truth is that the consumers are the bananas and the stores are the gorillas. Gorillas need bananas to survive. So the gorillas come up with all kinds of tricks and schemes (they call it marketing) to attract more bananas. Offering deep discounts is their favorite "trick." And the bananas fall for it every time. They line up to get eaten by the gorillas, who get fatter and fatter and happier and happier.

Meanwhile, the bananas get skinnier and skinnier and more and more frustrated. They hang from the tree trying to figure out why they can't get ahead in life. Then a gorilla shouts, "Buy it cheaper over here!" And the bananas get all excited, jump off the tree and line up to get eaten all over again.

Wake Up and Smell the Coffee!

Attention, all you consumers! I've got an announcement for you:

Your consumer plan isn't working!

You've been conditioned to believe that you're saving money when you buy at discount, but all you're really doing is buying liabilities instead of assets... working longer hours in order to buy more discounted merchandise... and piling up credit card debt at a 20%-plus interest rate so that you can keep the producers fat and happy.

Wake up, consumers! You've bought into the wrong plan! And can you guess who sold you that plan? That's right — the producers! When you compare the Consumer Plan to the Producer Plan, it's easy to see why the producers want to keep things just as they are. The chart below tells the tale:

Consumer Plan	Vs	Producer Plan
1. Spend money		1. Make money
2. Have a job		2. Own the company
3. Salary capped		3. Unlimited income
4. Deeper in debt		4. Financially free
5. Old-economy thinking		5. New-economy thinking
6. Increased liabilities		6. Increased assets
7. Short-term "savings"		7. Long-term wealth

The advent of e-commerce just magnifies these two plans. On-line consumers are getting all excited because spending is easier and cheaper than ever before. And on-line producers are excited because they can grow bigger and fatter with less effort.

In fact, the Internet has spawned a new breed of producer — the King Kong of commerce! Like the monsters in the black and white science-fiction movies, the e-cloud has descended on the baby Internet gorilla, mutating him so that he grows faster and bigger than any gorilla who ever lived! As for the bananas, they're getting smaller and smaller, while King Kong is getting bigger and bigger — and he's only a baby!

What's a consumer to do?

The Producer Advantage

Producers enjoy a lot of advantages in life that consumers miss out on. Like it or not, money has its privileges. As a consumer, here are some questions you need to ask yourself:

Wouldn't it be great to live where you wanted to live... instead of where you could afford? Big producers get to live where they want in grand style. What about you?

Wouldn't it be great to pay cash for a new luxury car every year?... instead of having to finance a used car for five years?

Wouldn't it be great to send your children away to a top-notch university?... instead of having them live at home while they attend the local junior college?

Wouldn't it be great to "retire" from your job and enjoy financial freedom when you're 35 or 45?.. instead of retiring from your job at 65 and living off a small pension and Social Security?

The truth is, producers get to choose how they live, while consumers get their lifestyles chosen for them. So I ask you, which would you rather be? A prosperous producer? Or a cash-strapped consumer?

Here's the bottom line: If you want to have what producers have... and live like producers live... *you have to start thinking and acting like producers think and act*!

The Downside of Becoming a Producer

The question becomes, "How do I become a bigger producer of wealth?" There are a couple of ways to do that. One is to do what .001% of the population does and start your own high-profit business from scratch. It can be done. Sam Walton of Wal-Mart fame did it. And so have hundreds of other legendary businessmen and women.

But let's face it, for every Sam Walton in the world, there are millions of us average consumers. The chances of you or me founding and growing a worldwide chain of discount stores (or setting up the next Amazon.com on the Internet) is one in a zillion. It takes millions of dollars... boundless ambition... and rare intelligence to do what these guys did.

Truth is, you and I have about as good a chance of becoming the next Michael Jordan as we do of becoming the next Sam Walton.

Pro-sumer Plan: Producing Wealth by Buying Smarter

But there is a way that 99.999% of people can *"have what producers have"* without investing millions. By learning, practicing, and teaching a system of wealth creation called pro-suming, average people can position themselves to create above-average income.

Pro-suming is a natural way for average people to create above-average wealth. Why? Because when we pro-sume, we leverage our skills and abilities as consumers, and if there's one thing most people are good at, it's consuming!

What we're NOT so good at is producing wealth. However, when we pro-sume, we partner up with a proven producer. As pro-sumers, our job is to buy products and services from the producer and to refer those products and services to people we know. The producer's job is to manufacture, warehouse, and ship those products.

The producer compensates us by paying us rebates and referral fees. We compensate the producer by increasing the demand for their products. It's a win/win. We pro-sumers keep doing what we're good at. The producer keeps doing what they're good at. And everybody makes money. *What a great concept!*

By entering into a pro-sumer partnership with a producer, we can enjoy all of the benefits of being a producer without incurring any of the liabilities. As pro-sumers, we get to make money while we spend money. Average people who want to create more wealth for themselves and their families *don't have to stop consuming. They need to start pro-suming*!

Pro-suming is a consumer's dream come true, as evidenced by the chart below comparing the Producer Plan with the Pro-sumer plan:

Producer Plan Vs	*Pro-sumer Plan*
1. Employees	1. No employees
2. Huge overhead	2. Low overhead
3. Offices, distribution	3. Home-based business centers
4. Expensive e-Commerce site	4. Computer with Internet access
5. Huge advertising budget	5. Word-of-mouth marketing
6. Divide profits with owners & shareholders	6. Keep all the profits for yourself

The best news is that the Internet has made it easier than ever for consumers to join the Pro-sumer Revolution.

Being a pro-sumer means directing traffic to your corporate partner, and then teaching others to do the same. Which means you don't have to sit on the sideline and watch producers get rich on the e-commerce explosion. *And just think — as an on-line pro-sumer, you can position yourself to get rich right along with them!*

PART THREE

THE CONSUMER MENTALITY

Over the years stores have come up with scores of proven strategies to entice us to spend more money, including deep discounts... easy credit... clever advertising... and creative store displays and product placement.

Consumers, on the other hand, are naive and unsuspecting, making us easy targets for stores to manipulate us into spending more.

The result? Stores are making record profits, while consumers are racking up record debt.

4

EITHER WAY, YOU PAY!

There is hardly anything in the world that some men can't make a little worse and sell a little cheaper, and the people who consider price only are this man's lawful prey.

— John Ruskin
English art critic and historian

U ntil recently, I'd never shopped at a discount buyers' club. At the urging of friends and relatives, I decided to check out a local discount store. Rest assured I won't be going back!

I won't mention the name of the buyers' club I went to, but from the outside it looked like an airplane hanger. Only bigger. And uglier. As my wife, Jeanne, and I walked to the entryway, we couldn't help but notice the litter in the parking lot. It looked like the aftermath of a tailgate party for the Superbowl. Two overflowing trash cans surrounded by smoldering cigarette butts guarded the entrance.

"If the front of the store looks like this," I said to Jeanne, "what does the back of the store look like?"

"I don't want to think about it," she said with a cringe. "But I guarantee we won't be buying fresh food here."

The inside of the warehouse resembled a Red Cross relief center. The concrete aisles were lined with giant metal shelves stacked to the rafters with cardboard boxes big enough to ship a compact car. We had to walk two city blocks to get to the canned food section. Sure enough, the prices were fantastically low! No wonder: Baked beans were in 10-pound containers. Tuna came in 96-ounce cans. And ketchup came in five-pound cans (not bottles, mind you. CANS!).

We managed to negotiate a barrel of pickles off a shelf without dropping it, and headed for the checkout. Surprise! The store didn't furnish grocery bags, and we didn't think to bring any. Not a problem. We could just roll the pickles out to the car. If only I'd brought a forklift so I could get them in the trunk....

You Get What You Pay For

I suppose wholesale clubs are great places to shop if you're the cook at a fraternity house or the comptroller of a boarding school. But for most people, the trade-off just doesn't make sense. Sure, you may save a few bucks in the short run. But the shopping experience is so unpleasant and the container sizes are so huge that, in the end, it's just not worth it.

Shopping experiences like these serve to remind us that *you get what you pay for*. You may get a *lower price*, but *you pay for it* with inconvenience... drab surroundings... or lousy service (and more often than not, all three!).

That's why I say, "Either way, you pay."

When people talk about the price of something, they usually mean the amount of money they agree to pay in exchange for a product or service. But I have a different definition of the word "price." Here's mine: *Price is what you have to give up to get what you want.*

Think about it. When I bought a five-gallon container of pickles at the wholesale club, the price was $5 cheaper than if I had bought five, one-gallon containers at the local supermarket. But look at what I had to *give up* to get that price:

I had to drive half way across town and back to get to the warehouse, which meant I *gave up at least an hour of my day*. I *gave up talking to the friendly cashiers* at my local market. And I *gave up the assistance of the bag boy* who carries our groceries out to the car.

What did I get in return for my $5 savings? I got unsmiling cashiers... no grocery bags... and a long walk around an ugly warehouse. In short, I gave up a pleasant shopping experience at a convenient supermarket for an unpleasant shopping experience half way across town. I gave up all that to save five lousy dollars. Now do you see what I mean when I say, *price is what you give up to get what you want*?

Drive a Yugo and Cook at Home

If money were the only cost in our buying decisions, then everyone would drive a Yugo and cook at home every night, isn't that true? So why don't we? Because we'd have to *give up so many wonderful intangibles for those rock-bottom prices, that's why*.

Either way, you pay.

Did you know that back in the 1960s, only 6% of the meals were eaten outside the home? Today 60% of the meals are eaten out, and that percentage goes up every year. Is it because it's cheaper to eat out? Of course not. We eat out so often because it's more convenient. It saves us time. Someone waits on us. And there are no dishes to wash afterward. The cost of the food itself is 30% of the final bill. The other 70% covers the intangibles, such as atmosphere... convenience... service... and so on. Yet three or four days a week, we gladly "give up" our hard-earned money in exchange for those intangibles.

Value Vs. Cost

Have you ever heard the phrase "value added" used to describe a product or service? Value added means the manufacturer or seller has included some worthwhile intangibles in their pricing. For example, a computer maker that adds "free" software or "free" on-line service is a value-added manufacturer. Most successful businesses understand that value is more important than cost, so they build their brand names around *adding more value*, as opposed to *lowering the cost*.

Rolex watches are a perfect example. Rolex watches keep very accurate time. Timex watches are just as accurate. Yet you could buy 1,000 Timex watches for the price of one Rolex. If both brands are equally reliable, what accounts for the huge price differential? In a word, the difference in cost between a Rolex and a Timex is an intangible called "status." Rolex wearers are announcing to the world that they can afford not only the necessities of life, but the luxuries. A Rolex isn't about telling time as much as it's about telling the world you're successful. And Rolex owners willingly pay thousands of dollars for the "added value."

Starbucks coffee is another example of people paying far more for the intangibles than they do for the product itself. When Starbucks customers pay $3 for 25 cents worth of coffee beans, they're paying 12 times what they would pay to drink that coffee at home — 12 *times*! Yet they line up for the privilege.

Do they feel ripped off? No! To the contrary, most Starbucks customers are repeat customers. The truth is, people who frequent the local Starbucks aren't just looking to buy a cup of coffee, anymore than a person who buys a Rolex is looking for a watch. Starbucks customers understand they're paying for *the experience* that goes along with their cup of coffee. And they value that intangible so much that Starbucks keeps expanding and increasing profits year after year.

Cheaper Is Not Necessarily Better

What do you think would happen if a no-frills, deep-discount coffee shop offering the same gourmet coffee as Starbucks for $1 per cup instead of $3 opened up next door to every Starbucks store in the world? Would it drive Starbucks out of business?

No way, or some enterprising entrepreneur would have already done it. *The point is that cheaper is not necessarily better*. The same people who will drive 20 miles to the local discount warehouse to save $5 on five gallons of pickles will stop at a Starbucks on their way back and plunk down $10 to buy two cups of coffee and a day-old cookie. Go figure....

Don't Be Penny Wise and Pound Foolish

As a nation of consumers, we've been conditioned to think that we're "smart shoppers" when we buy things on sale or at deep discount. Unfortunately, *we forget to factor in all the things we had to give up to get the lower price.*

The competition between the number one and two tire makers, Michelin and Goodyear, teaches us the lesson that buying cheap is not synonymous with buying smart.

Here's what happened:

For 42 years, Goodyear was the number one tire manufacturer in the world. They were so proud of their leading position that they sent the Goodyear blimp to major sporting events all across the country. For miles around people could look up and see the Goodyear blimp floating over their city displaying this giant message: *"Goodyear. Number 1 in Tires!"*

Only a few short years ago, Michelin was ranked number seven in sales worldwide, far behind industry leader Goodyear. Because Goodyear was a high-volume seller, there was no way Michelin could compete with Goodyear by offering the lowest price. The fact was Michelin's tires cost more, but for good reason — they were a better product.

The leaders at Michelin wisely decided to let Goodyear have the market for the cheapest tires. Michelin was confident they could become the number one tire seller in the world by concentrating on quality and innovation, instead of low cost. Michelin's biggest challenge was how best to deliver the message that, when it came to tires, cheaper is definitely NOT better!

That's when Michelin launched one of the most successful advertising campaigns in history. They produced a series of commercials featuring smiling babies sitting inside their tires. The slogan that accompanied the ads packed a powerful message:

"Because you have a lot riding on your tires."

WOW! Did that ad campaign ever deliver! Viewers of the Michelin ads became instantly aware of the wisdom of buying smarter, not cheaper. I mean, who in their right mind would risk the lives of their family to save $100 on a set of tires? Michelin's campaign caught on with the public in a big way, and within five years, they overtook Goodyear as the number one tire manufacturer in the world! And they did it by promoting quality, not price.

You Have a Lot Riding on Your Buying Decisions

Michelin was right — we do have a lot riding on our tires, just as you have a lot riding on ALL of your buying decisions. The Michelin ads really bring home the value of intangibles — especially health and safety.

But what about our *financial* health and safety?... we have a lot riding on our financial security, too, don't we?

The truth of the matter is, if we have enough money, we don't have to concern ourselves with buying the cheapest tires... or the cheapest anything, for that matter.

When multi-billionaire Bill Gates was building his 40,000-square-foot mansion on a lake in Seattle, do you think he really cared if the contractor "saved" 20% on the drywall? I mean, Gates is worth $100 billion! Do you think his wife drives to three different discount stores looking for the best price on Pampers? *Let's get real!*

I ask you — do you *really* want to spend the rest of your life driving from store to store in order to save a few bucks? Given the choice, wouldn't you prefer to use your valuable time to create wealth and build financial freedom?

When people shop for deep discounts, what is it they're REALLY after? — saving a few bucks in the short run? Or are they REALLY after financial freedom in the long run? I say smart people are REALLY after financial freedom in the long run.

What about you?

One last question: If I could show you a way to create financial independence by paying a fair and reasonable price for goods and services (instead of paying the cheapest price), would you change your buying habits?

Smart buyers, such as the rich dad in the book, *Rich Dad, Poor Dad*, answer "yes" to that question.

What about you?

5

THE STORE IS NOT YOUR FRIEND!

Your emotions while shopping have been hijacked.

— Terri Goldstein
Retail marketing consultant

There's a joke I like tell to my marketing students when I want to illustrate the fine line between good marketing and bad ethics. The joke goes like this:

A man walked into a veterinarian's office and asked to see the doctor.

"I have a real problem with my race horse," the man said.

"What seems to be the problem?" asked the vet.

"Well, sometimes he walks around just fine. But other times he walks with a terrible limp. What do you suggest I do?"

"*Next time he's walking fine,*" replied the vet, "*sell him!*"

My students always laugh, but it doesn't take us long to get into a serious discussion about the concept of truth in advertising. I explain that it's wrong to deliberately deceive customers, which is why the veterinarian's comment was not to be taken seriously. Bad ethics is bad business, plain and simple.

On the other hand, it's good business to present a product in its best light. There's nothing unethical about persuading people that your product will make them happier... or healthier... or wealthier... or prettier... or whatever. That's what marketing is all about — positioning a product in the best light so that consumers will want to own it.

The Store Is Not Your Friend

Stores are masters at presenting themselves in the best light. They're masters at making us feel comfortable and right at home — just like a friend.

For example, stores go out of their way to provide *friendly service*. Supermarket chains *build in our neighborhoods* — just like a friend. Big discount chains *make themselves available to us* by opening early and closing late, seven days a week — just like a friend. In our fast-paced, ever-changing world, it's *comforting* to know stores will always be there when we need them — just like a friend.

But make no mistake, stores aren't what they appear to be! Truth be known, every store has a "hidden agenda" that we sometimes lose sight of, namely, *stores are in business to make a profit*. The more stores can convince us they're our friend, the more likely we are to keep coming back and spending more money.

That's not friendship. That's marketing.

That's why I say, "The store is not your friend." Stores just *act* friendly so that we'll be more disposed to give them our money. Don't get me wrong — I'm not saying friendly service is a bad thing. Fact is, friendly service is a good thing. *But to stores, friendly service is a function of marketing.* And the purpose of marketing is to sell more products so that the stores can earn more profits.

Masters at Marketing

Over the years, stores have become masters at marketing. Through trial and error and research, store owners have discovered which "tricks of the trade" are most effective at manipulating shoppers into spending more and more of their hard-earned money.

Research shows, for example, that shoppers spend more at stores that feature pretty displays... offer deep discounts... hand out free samples... and hire friendly employees. At first glance, it looks to us consumers as if stores go out of their way for our benefit.

But stores don't go out of their way to make you feel good because they really and truly *care* about you as a person. *The simple truth is, they go out of their way to make you feel good so that you'll give them more of your money!* They care about you, all right, in the same way that a casino cares about gamblers. As long as the money holds out, the customer is the king. No money, no throne. Nothing personal, you understand. It's only business.

The store may *act friendly* in order to put you in a better spending mood. But make no mistake about it, stores are in business to make profits, not friends. Acting friendly isn't deceptive. Acting friendly isn't unethical. Acting friendly is just marketing... it's just business, you understand — good business!

Why do you think Wal-Mart hires greeters to welcome you? A friendly greeting makes you feel wanted, doesn't it? Makes you feel appreciated. Makes you feel like a person instead of a number.

"*How are you today?*" smiling Wal-Mart greeters may ask. "*May I get you a shopping cart? Anything I can help you with today? Enjoy your visit.*" When friendly Wal-Mart greeters — usually senior citizens who remind you of a kindly grandparent — smile and ask how you're doing, it just lifts your spirits, doesn't it?

But wait a second — if you walked past one of those greeters at a bus stop, do you think they'd engage you in the same light-hearted conversation? Not a chance. So why do they greet you so enthusiastically when you enter a Wal-Mart? *Because it's their job, that's why! They get paid to act friendly!*

Greeters are trained to smile and ask you scripted questions in a friendly voice. At the end of each week, they get a paycheck. Nothing personal, you understand. Only business. And what good business it is. Wal-Mart's "friendly service" is one of the reasons it's the largest, most profitable retailer in the world.

Tricks of the Trade

Having a smiling senior citizen "greet" you at the door is only one of hundreds of marketing "tricks of the trade" that stores use to entice customers to spend more money. Now, when I use the term "tricks of the trade," I don't want to imply that stores are unethical. They're just very good at presenting themselves and their products so that you want to buy them — right there and then!

Good marketing is like dating. If you finally got a date with your "dream companion," you'd make every effort to look your best and be on your best behavior. You'd be polite. Attentive. Friendly. You'd select just the right out-fit and shine your shoes for this special occasion. Putting your best foot forward isn't the same as being deceptive. Sprucing up for a first date is just one of the "tricks of the trade" of the dating game, and these tricks help you accomplish your goal — getting a second, third and fourth date!

Stores are the same way. When a store creates an attractive display of merchandise, the store isn't being deceptive. They're just using one of the many "tricks of the trade" to help them accomplish *their* goal — which is to get you to buy products and services again and again.

The Store Is an Expert — You Are an Amateur

Over the years, stores have gotten very good at accomplishing their goal of separating us from our money. *Very good*! In fact, stores have gotten a lot better at *selling* than customers have gotten at *buying*.

You see, stores are EXPERTS AT SELLING, while most of us are AMATEURS AT BUYING. That's because selling is a store's full-time business. It's their reason for existence. It's what they study... think about... and do all day, every day.

The average customer, on the other hand, only shops from time to time. We're anything but experts. Stores have all these proven "tricks of the trade" that entice us to spend money. And what do we have? A shopping list and a car parked at an expired meter. *It's no contest!*

The relationship between the store and its customers reminds me of a relationship I had with our dog Fitch. She loved to escape from the fenced-in backyard. When I left for work in the morning, I would let her loose in our backyard. When I came home from work, Fitch would be waiting for me in the front yard!

After several months, I came to a realization. I would

49

never be able to keep Fitch penned up because Fitch made it her mission in life to escape from the backyard. In my spare time, I'd patch together a new barricade to keep her in. Fitch, on the other hand, made escaping her full-time occupation. It became her reason for living. And no matter what new barricade I came up with, it was only a matter of time before Fitch found a way around it.

Full-Time Stores Vs. Part-Time Shoppers

The "game" that I played with Fitch is like the game you play with the retail store. You and I can only spend a few minutes a day thinking about shopping smart. We have jobs to work at. Families to raise. Lives to live. Shopping is only a part-time activity for us.

However, like Fitch, the store's job is full-time! The store has one thing on its mind all day long, every single day of the week, year in and year out. As soon as we customers erect a barricade to buying, such as resolving to control spending by not making another major purchase for at least a year — then the stores find a way over, under, or through our barricade of resistance, with offers like these: NO PAYMENTS FOR 12 MONTHS!

The simple truth is that we can't possibly keep up with all of the gimmicks a store can come up with to get more and more of our money. Their mission is to get in our pockets. When we enter a store, we're on their turf. Talk about a home court advantage! When we walk into a retail store, it's like walking into the lion's den armed with a popgun.

We haven't got a chance!

Why We Buy

Today stores have gotten marketing down to a science — literally! Just as anthropologists study other cultures, retail anthropologists study shoppers to discover how they go about making their buying decisions. A retail scientist named Paco Underhill spent thousands of hours observing... tracking... filming... taping... and interviewing shoppers. He published his findings in a best-selling book called *Why We Buy: The Science of Shopping*, and the book quickly became a must-read for retailers. The book reveals shoppers' buying patterns and tells retailers how they can dramatically increase in-store sales by adopting some simple strategies.

For example, thousands of hours of videotaping revealed that most people turn to their right when they enter a store. Armed with this knowledge, airports are now locating their gift shops on the right and the foodcourts on the left, knowing that people will turn right to spend money in the gift shop before grabbing a bite to eat.

Manipulating Your Emotions

In the next few pages, I'll identify some of the other "tricks" that stores use to get you to buy more merchandise. Some of the material you are about to read comes from Underhill's book. Some of it comes from an exposé hosted by Barbara Walters on 20/20, ABC's weekly news program. And some of it comes from my years of experience as a marketing professor.

Thousands of profitable retail stores use these strategies to increase their bottom line. On the other hand, only one in a million customers knows they're being "tricked." The vast majority of customers are innocent geese just waiting to be plucked. Underhill sums up the contest between savvy stores and unsuspecting shoppers this way:

> *More and more purchasing decisions are being made on the premises of the store itself. Customers have disposable income and open minds, and they're giving in to impulses. The role of merchandising has never been greater.*

Sounds like the deck is stacked against the shopper in favor of the store, doesn't it? No wonder that 70% of our in-store purchases are impulse buys! Warehouse stores are the masters at enticing shoppers to make impulse buys, which is why, according to *Forbes* magazine, the average shopper spends $50 more at a warehouse store versus a supermarket.

Ironically, shoppers think they save money when they shop at warehouses, but *they end up spending more money*! As I said, stores are the pros, and we're the amateurs. And there's *no way we can beat them at their game on their playing field*. NO WAY!

Now let's take a look at 10 common strategies that stores use to stack the deck and trick customers into buying more merchandise.

Trick 1: Keep 'em in the store longer

Underhill says that the single biggest factor in determining how much a shopper will spend is how long they stay in the store. With this in mind, stores do whatever they can to slow you down! They use soft, soothing music and lighting to relax you and slow down your pace. One lighting consultant's goal was to reduce the number of times shoppers blink from 30 to 14 blinks per minute! Why? Research shows that the less you blink, the more relaxed you are and the slower you go. Ever wonder why the aisles in the produce section wind all over the place? So you will slow down and, you guessed it, buy more!

Trick 2: Increase the number of impulse buys

Research shows that more than two out of every three items we purchase in stores are impulse buys! Knowing this, retailers set up their stores to encourage shoppers to buy more stuff on the spur of the moment. The classic example is the candy display at the checkout counter. But stores set up impulse buying opportunities all over the store. For example, next time you're in the produce section of your supermarket, notice how shortcake and whipped cream are conveniently displayed next to the fresh strawberries.

Trick 3: Sell to the kids, and the parents will buy

Underhill's video cameras showed that dog treats and cereal were often picked out by children. The cameras caught children trying to climb the shelves to reach the boxes. When stores moved the cereal and pet treats to middle shelves where children could reach them easily, sales went up overnight! Gives new meaning to the expression, "Like taking candy from a baby," doesn't it?

Trick 4: Exploit the human element

According to Underhill, the number one thing shoppers look at is other people. That's why some of the most effective signs in fast-food restaurants are the ones sitting at eye level on top of cash registers. When customers look at the cashier, they invariably see a sign. Smart sign placement is a surefire way to increase sales.

Trick 5: Mix up the merchandise

Ever notice how many different kinds of soups are on display in the soup section of the supermarket? There must be 100 varieties. With that many different flavors, you would think stores would alphabetize the soups so that we could find the ones we were after more easily. But stores mix the different soups up on purpose. Why? So that shoppers will have to scan all over the shelf for the flavor they're after. In the meantime, their eyes light on all kinds of specialty soups they never knew existed. That's how a can of Fiesta Nacho and Cheese soup ends up in the shopping cart along with the Chicken Noodle soup you were after.

Trick 6: Silence the cash registers
Are you old enough to remember when cash registers used to announce your total bill with the noisy alarm, "*Cha-a-ching!*"? No such racket at the checkout counter today, for that noisy old cash register has been replaced by a nearly silent one that hums instead of clangs. Purring cash registers and buy-now, pay-later credit cards soften the impact of spending, which means higher volume per customer for stores (and higher credit card debt for consumers).

Trick 7: Communicate in sign language
Underhill tells his clients to stop thinking of their space as a store and to start thinking of it as a three-dimensional TV commercial. In effect, the store is a walk-in container for the words, thoughts, messages, and ideas that stores want shoppers to receive. Well-placed signs and strong messages can dramatically increase a store's profits. "If everything inside the store is working right," Underhill says, "the signs grab shoppers' attention and induce them to look and shop and buy some more. And just as with scripting and directing a TV commercial, the job with signs is to figure out what to say and when and how to say it."

Trick 8: Make 'em walk but not wait
Buyers who are on a mission won't take the time to

shop until after they have completed their task. That's why "drug stores" like Walgreens put pharmacies in the rear of the store. Customers seeking to pick up a prescription will march to the back, ignoring every sign and display until their mission is accomplished. It's futile to try to sell them anything until after they've accomplished their task. Once customers have received their prescription, they must walk all the way back to the front of the store. Savvy stores place signs and displays facing the back of the store so that people returning from the pharmacy will be tempted with impulse buys.

Trick 9: Feed 'em for "free" and they'll line up to pay for it

Watch out for those friendly people in supermarkets handing out "free" samples. Studies have shown that up to 90% of shoppers who try certain products will buy them. Why the astronomical closing rate? "Umm-m, that's delicious" will often lead to an impulse buy. Guilt plays a factor with shoppers who feel obligated to buy a product that they just received for "free." Stores don't care how sampling works. They just know it increases sales. We've all heard there is no such thing as a free lunch. Next time you're tempted to taste a sample, remember there's no such thing as a free sample, either.

Trick 10: Start 'em young

As the twig is bent, so grows the tree. Likewise, as consumers are bent, so goes their spending. Stores are like tobacco companies — they want to start you young and hook you for life! That's why so many stores, especially supermarkets, are designed with children in mind. Where is the junk cereal displayed? About four feet off the ground, right at a child's eye level! Same with cookies and snack foods. The supermarket in my neighborhood designed a tight turn in the frozen food section so that when I wheel around the corner, ice cream is displayed in huge glass freezers on both sides of the aisle! You can hear the kids begging their parents for "Double Fudge Chunky Monkey" three aisles away. Did I mention the bakery gives away free cookies to kids? So considerate of them....

These are only 10 of the hundreds of "tricks" that stores use to induce shoppers to spend freely and often. And as competition increases, you can bet that stores will get better at manipulating our emotions in order to increase their profits.

Breaking the Consumer Cycle

I don't know about you, but when I first learned about some of the tricks stores use to get us to spend more than we intend, I felt a lot like Pavlov's dog. Pavlov rang a bell, put out a plate of food, and conditioned the dog to salivate. Likewise, the store sets up a display, hands out a free sample, and we're conditioned to buy.

Stores have conditioned us to consume our wealth. The more we consume, the more they create wealth. It's an endless cycle. And the only way to break the consumer cycle is to change our buying habits. Instead of allowing stores to condition us to consume, what if we conditioned ourselves to pro-sume? Now there's a concept!

What if we transferred our buying of regular monthly consumables from the local store — "They-Mart" — to our own store — "My-Mart?"

What if we re-conditioned ourselves to become producers of wealth by thinking like the store instead of spenders of wealth by thinking like consumers?

What if we reduced our impulse buying by shopping from the comfort of our own home, instead of driving to the local store and volunteering to be manipulated into buying things we don't really need or want?

What if we broke out of the negative-cash-flow consumer cycle and replaced it with a positive-cash-flow pro-sumer cycle?

What if we thought and acted like the store and taught others to do the same?

If we did these things, and persuaded enough people to join us, we'd create a Pro-sumer Revolution that would change the way people live, work, and create wealth, wouldn't we?

And if we did that, the store would become more than a friend. It would become part of the family because we would own it! And ownership, my friend, is what pro-suming is all about!

6

THE ROAD TO DEBT
IS PAVED WITH
DISCOUNTS

---

*I'll have all the money I'll ever need if I
die by four o'clock.*

— Henny Youngman
Comedian

"*Lassie, come home!*"
Every Sunday night during the mid-1950s and
'60s, millions of North Americans would tune
their TV sets to CBS and watch Lassie's owner, "Timmy,"
played by adorable child-actor Jon Provost, open each epi-
sode of the classic TV series with this familiar refrain:
"*Lassie, come home!*"
Lassie was one of the longest-running shows in the his-

tory of TV, and it made Provost a millionaire before he was even a teenager.

You'd think that Provost's financial head start would put him on easy street for the rest of his life. But 40 years later, a poorer but wiser Provost tells an all-too-common story of someone with more money than sense.

"I pretty much partied my money away," Provost says matter-of-factly.

Provost says his teenage spending spree started when he dropped $6,000 for a sports car. Within a decade, he managed to consume his way through several million dollars. Today Provost and two other ex-child stars — Brandon Cruz, who starred in the 1970s show *The Courtship of Eddie's Father*; and Paul Petersen, Jeff on *The Donna Reed Show*, are touring the talk show circuit telling interviewers how bad buying habits led them to squander away their Hollywood fortunes.

I'm sure they bought a lot of their stuff at discount. As their bank accounts dwindled, they probably "saved" a lot of money by buying their "toys" cheaper. But no matter how deep the discounts, when people over-consume, it's only a matter of time before the "out-go" overtakes the income.

How to Win — and Lose — the Lottery

"When I win the lottery, I'll...."

We've all heard that line a million times before. Like most people, Paul Scott Cooney used to kid around about winning the lottery, too. Then one day it happened. His one-in-a-zillion chance came true! At age 26, Cooney won over $20 million in the Florida lottery. He was set for life. Or so he thought.

Ten years later, Cooney appeared in bankruptcy court negotiating a plan to pay off $5 million in debt. What happened to his windfall of a million dollars a year for 20 years? He spent it on lavish living, and he shunned investments in favor of purchasing countless liabilities, such as cars, motorcycles, and expensive gifts for friends and family.

Now, I bet Cooney negotiated some really good discounts during those 10 years of free spending. When people buy furniture by the semi-truck load and motorcycles three at a time, you'd better believe they got some great discounts.

But discounts or no discounts, *consuming reduces assets.* The balance in a bank account may go down a little more slowly when people buy at a discount — *but it still goes down!* It doesn't matter if you're a millionaire child actor... or a lucky lottery winner... or a widow on welfare, *consuming diminishes assets.* It's just that simple. People tell themselves they're "saving" money when they buy at discount. But all they're really saving is a little time until they milk the cow dry.

Over-Spending Is the Rule, Not the Exception.

You might think the ex-child actor and lucky lottery winner are exceptions, not the rule. Frankly, it's the other way around. AS A RULE, NORTH AMERICANS ARE CONSUMING THEMSELVES INTO THE POORHOUSE!

Let's take a look at some sobering facts.

- *More than 1.2 million people filed for bankruptcy in the U.S. in 1998* — and the number is increasing every year despite a booming economy.

- *The average American household owed about $7,000 in credit card debt (at a rate between 12% and 22%), and credit card debt more than doubled from 1990 to 2000.*

- *Americans work the longest hours in the industrial-*

ized world. In 1997, Americans worked 8 HOURS MORE PER WEEK than they did in 1980.

- According to a *USA Today* survey, *54% of Americans say it would take three months or less to fall behind in bill payments if they lost their job today.*

- Household borrowing stands at a record $6.3 trillion — *almost a 50% jump in the past five years.*

- If Social Security disappeared tomorrow, *half of all senior citizens, starting tomorrow, would be forced to live in poverty.*

These facts indicate that people are working harder, but they're falling farther and farther into debt. It's like the bumper sticker I see from time to time: *"The harder I works, the behinder I gets."*

The answer to creating more wealth is to spend smarter, not work harder! If more people understood how to create more wealth by buying smarter instead of spending their wealth by buying cheaper, they could create true financial security for themselves and their families.

It's Never Too Late to Make a U-Turn

I think most people spend themselves into the poorhouse because they aren't aware of an alternative way of consuming. They've been taught that they actually "save" money when they buy products at deep discounts. I truly believe that if more people learned about the power of pro-suming, we'd have fewer bankruptcies and more high-income earners.

The road to debt may be paved with discounts, but people don't have to stay on that road. They can choose to turn around and head the other direction toward financial freedom. The choice to remain a consumer — or to change direction and become a pro-sumer — is yours and yours alone.

Choose wisely. You'll never regret it.

7

WHAT IS IT YOU REALLY WANT — DEEPER DISCOUNTS? ... OR MORE TIME?

We all know that in our professional and personal lives, time is the only commodity worth anything anymore.
— Scott Reamer
Market analyst of technology stocks

Here's an old joke that could serve as a parable for modern times:
A man named Chuck loved fishing more than anything else in the world. Every winter he would sink into a deep depression because all of the lakes were frozen over for months at a time.

Then a friend told him about ice fishing.

"What a great idea!" Chuck shouted. "I'll go first thing

in the morning."

Bright and early the next day, Chuck lugged all his gear to a smooth stretch of ice. He cut a hole in the ice with an ax, baited up his hook, and dropped in his line. Then he waited patiently.

Chuck fished for two hours without a bite. Suddenly, a loud, deep voice from above broke the silence.

"There are no fish in here!"

Undeterred, Chuck fished on. About an hour later, he heard the booming voice again.

"There are no fish in here!"

Chuck hadn't fished in months, so he wasn't easily discouraged. He kept staring at his line, patiently waiting for a fish to strike. Another hour passed.

"THERE ARE NO FISH IN HERE!"

Chuck couldn't ignore the booming voice any longer. He covered his head with his arms and asked meekly, "Are you God?"

"NO! I'M THE MANAGER OF THE ICE SKATING RINK."

Fishing in the Wrong Place for Happiness

It occurs to me that the story of Chuck the ice fisherman is a fitting parable for so many people today who, instead of casting their line for fish, are casting about for happiness and fulfillment. But they're like the fisherman in the ice rink — they're passionate about their mission, but they're fishing in the wrong place! Allow me to explain.

We live in a consumer society, so most people are fishing for happiness by trying to buy more and more things at cheaper and cheaper prices. But the simple truth is, people will never be able to "catch" happiness by "fishing" at discount malls or by buying merchandise on sale. When people seek to buy happiness by shopping for discounts, they might as well be ice fishing in a skating rink.

If more people would step back and ask themselves, *"What is it I REALLY want? — deeper discounts?... Or more time?"...* they might be surprised to learn that spending their time shopping in order to acquire more things at cheaper prices is *not* what they really want out of life.

You see, people who shop for discounts are *spending their time in order to save money.* That's a big mistake because time is our most valuable possession! Happy, fulfilled people understand the value of time, so they don't spend time to save money — *they spend money to save time!*

Time — Not Discounts — Is What We Really Want

Just to make sure you understand the value of time vs. the value of money, I'd like you to put yourself in the following scenario:

I want you to imagine that you're in the prime of your life. You're happily married, have two terrific kids, lots of great friends, and two healthy parents you adore. You're on top of the world.

Then you receive some terrible news — you're dying of a terminal illness, and you only have one week to live.

That's the bad news.

The good news is you're the richest person in the world, worth $100 billion! The only thing that can save your life is a miracle drug developed by a mad scientist. The drug will cure you immediately, and you will live at least another 10 years, possibly more.

Now for the $100-billion question.

The mad scientist will sell you this drug under one condition. *You sign all your earthly possessions over to him!* He gets your mansion... your yachts... your businesses... your stocks... your bank accounts. He gets everything but your life, your family, and the skills and abilities that enabled you to earn $100 billion.

The scientist gives you one minute to decide — your

money or more time on earth. He's holding an ironclad contract transferring all of your worldly goods over to him. The clock is ticking — tick... tick... tick. If you sign the paper, all you would have left are your wits, your knowledge, your family, and at least 10 more years of great health.

Would you sign the contract transferring all your worldly assets over to this scientist in exchange for more time on Earth? Tick... tick... tick... five seconds to decide... four... three... two... one... *What is it you REALLY want?* More money? Or more time?

I don't know about you, but I'd sign that paper in a nanosecond! When you compare the value of money vs. the value of time, it's not even a contest. Time is far, far more valuable than money. It's not even close! We can always make more money. But we'll never be able to make more time. We've all been given 1,440 minutes a day in this life, no more, no less. Whether we squander time or honor time is up to each of us.

What Do Rich People Shop for? Discounts?... Or Convenience?

Rich people have always understood that time is more valuable than money. They take the expression, "Time is money" to heart, and they spend money to save time, rather than spending time to save money.

When Michael Jordan goes on a buying spree to furnish his new mansion, what do you think he and his wife are most concerned about — saving money by shopping at garage sales or the local discount furniture mart?... Or saving time by hiring a designer to do the shopping for them? In other words, do you think the Michael Jordans of the world shop for discounts?... or for convenience?

Now, I don't want to give you the impression that you have to be a zillionaire to spend money to save time. Nothing could be further from the truth. Middle class people own washers and dryers in their homes. Why? It saves us time. That's why the service economy has continued to grow by leaps and bounds — more and more people are spending money to save time. Instead of ironing clothes, we send them out to the dry cleaners. Instead of mowing the lawn each week, we hire a yard service. The list goes on and on.

But for some reason, most people still think that they're smart when they drive half an hour to shop at a discount store... stand in the checkout line for 20 minutes... endure rude clerks (if they can even find one)... and fight the traffic on the way home to "save" a few bucks on laundry detergent!

What's wrong with this picture?

Buying Time

When my wife, Jeanne, and I were first married, we recognized right away that time was more important than money. As a result, we decided that whenever possible, *we'd spend money to save time, and then use that time to enjoy our family*! We've never regretted that decision for a moment.

I remember when the guy next door bragged about "saving" $2,000 by painting his house himself instead of hiring a painting contractor. But my neighbor had to spend his vacation time to do the job! That's insane! While he was painting his house, I was in Disney World with Jeanne and the two kids, having the time of our lives. I wouldn't trade that experience and those memories for anything. Meanwhile, the neighbor who "saved" $2,000 by trading time for money was too tired in the evenings to play catch with his two boys. What a loss... and what a shame.

Ever heard the expression, "No one on his deathbed ever wished he'd spent more time in the office"? Well, no one on their deathbed ever wished they'd "saved" a few thousand dollars painting their own home... or mowing their own yard... instead of enjoying their kids while they were growing up.

"If you have enough money, you can buy someone else's time," says psychologist Robert Levine. "You can pay people to run your errands. Your time is worth more than their time." Jeanne and I didn't need a psychologist to tell us that. But thanks just the same, Dr. Levine.

How to "Save" Five Extra Years in Your Life

What if I could show you a way to "buy" an extra five years of pleasure and enjoyment in your life? Would you be interested? Impossible, you say. Not at all — I've already bought more than two years of time myself. Let me explain.

Let's say you're spending an hour or two a day to save a little money, when you could be using that time more productively by, say, working part-time from your home in order to build a high-income, home-based business... or spending more time playing Yahtzee with your kids... or working out at the gym.

At first glance, an hour or two a day doesn't sound like very much. But an hour or two a day adds up to 10 hours a week, which adds up to more than 500 hours a year! If you are awake 16 hours a day, 500 hours calculates to be about 31 days, or the equivalent of one month of extra time available to you each and every year!

So, by spending money to save time, we could save a month of time every year, correct? Which means every 12 years, we could save the equivalent of one year of our lives! If you start spending money to save time when you are 20 years old and you live to be 80, that's 60 months of time — or five years — that you could have saved!

Just think — you could add five years of productive,

quality, fun time to your life just by investing money to save time, instead of investing time to save money. How would you use that extra time? Would you play more golf with your friends? Would you spend more time with your spouse and children? Would you travel to exotic places? Would you start a part-time business? Or would you do all of the above?

Now are you beginning to see why I say saving time is more important than saving money shopping for discounts?

What If....

What if I could show you a way to have your cake and eat it, too?... a way not only to "save" money, but to earn money, while you save time?

Would that be a revolutionary concept worth learning about?

What if there were a way to buy products at a fair and reasonable price and have them delivered to your front door, instead of having to fight traffic... stand in checkout lines... clip coupons... or lug heavy bags of groceries half a mile across a crowded parking lot (only to discover you forgot where you parked the car)?

Would that be a revolutionary concept worth learning about?

What if there were a way you could open your own home-based business and earn anywhere from a couple hundred dollars a month working part-time from your home computer... to a couple hundred thousand dollars a year working full-time?

Would that be a revolutionary concept worth learning about?

That concept is alive and well — and is just waiting to be exploited by people like you and me. It's the marriage of Pro-sumer Power — buying smarter, not cheaper, and then teaching others to do the same — coupled with the power and convenience of the Internet.

This revolutionary concept is a combination of a 50-year-old proven industry called Referral Commerce, combined with the speed and efficiency of e-commerce. It's a concept my good friend Burke Hedges calls "e-ferral Commerce," and it's changing the way the world lives, works, and creates wealth.

The e-volution of Referral Commerce

E-ferral Commerce may not be a concept you've heard of before. Don't let that throw you. The Internet was a concept that most people hadn't heard of until the mid-'90s. But in less than five years, the Internet is the driving force behind a booming global economy and is creating more wealth than any industry in the history of the world.

When you marry the efficiency, speed, and reach of e-commerce with Pro-sumer Power, you create a revolutionary business model that will create billions of dollars for millions of people all over the world in the coming decade.

Now let's learn how this revolutionary concept called e-ferral Commerce can empower you to "turn e-commerce into Me-commerce" and *get what you REALLY want out of life.*

And what is it you *REALLY want out of life*?

More time, of course.

And more money to enjoy that time!

Just think — more time and more money. Now, that wouldn't be just *a* dream come true... that would be *your* dream come true!

PART FOUR

MY-MART.COM: THE CONVERGENCE OF PRO-SUMING AND E-COMMERCE

Free commerce has a long-standing tradition of paying referral fees to customers or vendors who bring in new business.

As more and more businesses open e-commerce sites, they are relying more and more on referrals to help them expand.

The convergence of pro-suming and e-commerce gives birth to a dynamic referral-based concept for wealth creation known as "e-ferral Commerce," a concept some experts are calling "The opportunity of the New Millennium!"

8

REFERRAL COMMERCE: PRO-SUMER POWER AT WORK

Opportunities can drop in your lap —
if you place your lap where opportunities
drop.

— Anonymous

A photo of Babe Ruth fills the TV screen as the announcer says:

"Babe Ruth was acquired for $125,000."

A photo of the Alaskan wilderness appears. The announcer says:

"Seward bought Alaska for two cents an acre."

A photo of the world's first computer appears. The announcer says:

"The first computer cost $485,744.02."

Then the word *"VALUE"* appears on the screen, followed by a photo of a new Mercedes. The announcer says:
"It isn't always what you pay. It's what you get in return."

The TV commercial for Mercedes makes a powerful point about value — namely, that price isn't necessarily synonymous with value. Buying smarter, not cheaper, means that you take more than just price into consideration. Asking the question, "What do I get in return for the price?" will reveal the true value of a product or service.

For example, there are a lot of cars cheaper than a Mercedes that will perform the same function, namely, to get you from point A to point B. But Mercedes owners will tell you *they get a lot in return for the extra cost*, such as comfort. Style. Resale value. Status. Safety. Reliability. And so on. The return that Mercedes owners get far outweighs the extra cost, which is why Mercedes owners are so loyal to the brand.

What Do Pro-sumers Get in Return?

The same goes for every purchase we make: *"It isn't always what you pay. It's what you get in return."* Think about it — when consumers buy products at discount, what do they get in return? *They get a liability that loses more and more value over time.* That's why you're lucky if someone pays you $200 for a two-year-old couch that cost you $2,000 new. Couches, like cars and clothes and most everything else we buy, are *depreciating liabilities*, as opposed to *increasing assets*, and liabilities can lose more than half their value as soon as they leave the showroom floor.

But look what happens when we think like pro-sumers, instead of consumers. Pro-sumers not only get the product or service, but, *in return, they get the opportunity to own their own business and earn money!* Pro-sumers may pay a little more on the front end for a product or service, but what they get in return — *opportunity* — far outweighs the extra cost, for pro-sumers have the opportunity to earn hundreds... thousands... yes, even millions of dollars by buying smarter and teaching others to do the same!

Adding Value with Referral Fees

We've all heard the expression, "You scratch my back, I'll scratch yours." In other words, you help me build my house, and I'll help you build your house. You help me make more money, and I'll help you make more money. The Latin term is *quid pro quo,* which means something for something.

Well, that's the concept behind pro-sumerism — you help your corporate partner grow by referring people to their products and services, and the company will compensate you by giving you better discounts... or by paying you a referral fee... or both. You not only get the product, you get the opportunity to own your own business and build assets. It's a win/win.

Referral fees have been around in one form or another since the beginning of commerce. Referral fees are a powerful, proven way to grow a business. For example, I have a friend who owns a residential real estate company. His office sells as many as 100 homes a month, which means each of the 100 new homeowners will be seeking out a mortgage company for a loan... a title company to help with the closing... and an insurance company to write new policies.

Now, let's say you owned a title company. Wouldn't it make good business sense to pay my realtor friend a small fee for any business he referred to you? Of course it would. It made good sense to my realtor friend, too. He sat down with the owner of the best title company in town and struck a deal. In exchange for referring all of his business to AAA Title, my friend received $50 per referral, which calculates to more than $50,000 a year in referral fees.

The beauty of this referral arrangement is that everybody comes out ahead. The realtor is happy because he makes money just for his word-of-mouth endorsement. The title company is happy because it gets 100 or so new customers a month without having to advertise. And the clients are happy because they get great service at a reasonable fee. That's the power of referrals — there's value added to every person involved in the transaction.

A Crash Course in Referral Commerce

In the late 1940s, a small vitamin company realized that most of their new business was coming from referrals — satisfied customers would recommend the vitamins to friends or family members, who in turn would refer the vitamins to their friends, and on and on down the line.

The owners made a daring decision that laid the groundwork for what has evolved into a $100-billion-a-year industry — they scrapped the company's traditional marketing plan and replaced it with Referral Commerce, a radical new marketing program based exclusively on referral fees. The more new business a customer brought in, the more money he or she could earn. It didn't take long for pro-sumer power to kick in. Customers quickly understood the wisdom of buying smarter, not cheaper, and teaching others to do the same.

As the customer base expanded, product sales grew, as did the size of the referral fees. A few of the more enterprising customer/partners were able to generate enough income from referrals to quit their traditional jobs and earn a living solely as professional pro-sumers.

Referral Commerce was off and running!

Over the next five decades, Referral Commerce exploded. Today there are literally millions of people worldwide partnering with Referral Commerce companies. By buying smarter, not cheaper, and then teaching others to do the same, Referral-based partners are earning anywhere from a few hundred dollars a month... to a few hundred thousand dollars a month — or more!

Exponential Growth: 1+1=4

The principle that makes Referral Commerce so explosive is a dynamic concept called "exponential growth," and it's the reason that Referral Commerce is the greatest opportunity in the world for average people to create above-average incomes.

A basic math lesson will demonstrate the power of exponential growth. We all know from elementary school how simple addition works: 1+1=2. Simple addition is an example of *linear growth*, that is, the growth is in a straight line.

Exponential growth, on the other hand, grows in multiples of two. Whereas linear growth can be represented by the equation, 1+1=2, exponential growth can be represented by the equation, $1+1=2^2$ (or 1+1=4). Obviously, exponential growth, also known as "the doubling concept," is far more dynamic than linear growth. Whereas linear growth is incremental and gradual, exponential growth is drastic and dramatic. And over time, exponential growth can create huge, huge numbers, as well as huge, huge profits!

How Referral Commerce Grows Exponentially

Here's how the exponential concept of 1+1=4 works in Referral Commerce: Let's say a friend asks you to try a vitamin supplement distributed through Referral Commerce. You love what the supplements do for you — you have more energy, and you lose a few pounds without really trying. You're living proof that the product works, and you feel good about referring the company's line of products to your acquaintances.

Let's assume that within a week of trying the product, you tell a friend about the product line and the opportunity to make some extra money, and he joins you in your new referral-based business.

The second week, you and your new business partner duplicate your efforts — that is, you refer the product and opportunity to another friend, and the first person you got to join you in your business refers the product to one of his friends.

By the end of the second week, you would have sponsored a second person into your business and your first partner would have sponsored one of his friends into his new business. You would now have a grand total of four people in your referral-based business — you... your two friends... and your first friend's new referral.

Now can you see why I say, 1+1=4?

If you and your referral continued to duplicate your efforts, week after week, the size of your referral organization would keep doubling, month after month, until your network numbered in the thousands! And all you did was refer one new person a week to the products and then teach everyone who joined you in the business to do the same.

Now, here's the really exciting part about Referral Commerce. Because you were the person who referred your first friend to the company's products, the company would not only offer you a discount on the products you would buy for your own consumption, but the company would also pay you referral fees or commissions on the products your friend buys... plus a commission on the products his friend buys... plus a commission on the products his friend's friends buy... and so on down the line.

If, during the course of a year or two, your referral organization grows to 100... or even 1,000 or more people, you could earn a commission on all of the products your organization buys during a given month. Considering that it's not uncommon for referral-based networks to number into the thousands — or *even hundreds of thousands of referral partners buying millions of dollars of products each and every month* — it's little wonder that thousands of people all over the world have achieved financial independence!

Referral Commerce and the Pro-sumer Mentality

Remember my definition of pro-suming? — *buying smarter, not cheaper, and then teaching others to do the same.* Well, that's a perfect definition for Referral Commerce, too — buying smarter, not cheaper, and teaching others to do the same!

You see, when you pro-sume in a Referral Commerce business, you position yourself to build assets while you buy — you position yourself to own your own business and create wealth by depositing checks from referral fees, rather than just writing checks for products and services.

Think about it. Wouldn't it be nice to *position yourself for income instead of out-go* when you buy? Since you have to buy consumable products such as shampoo, detergent, and groceries on a monthly basis anyway, doesn't it make sense to buy them from a company that will pay you a referral fee for any new business you bring them?

That's exactly what happens when you change your thinking from consumer thinking to pro-sumer thinking through Referral Commerce — you not only make money while you spend money, but you make even more money when your referral partners, and all of their partners, spend money.

The difference between pro-suming by buying from your own referral-based business and consuming by buying from a store is the difference between owning and renting... the difference between saving and spending... the difference between an asset and a liability... the difference between an investment and an expense.. and the difference between increasing your bank account and diminishing your bank account.

Sharing an Opportunity with Friends

I've noticed that everyone goes out of their way to share bargains with friends. We tell each other where to buy the cheapest gas. Where to buy the cheapest groceries. Where to buy the cheapest cars. Where to buy the cheapest airfares. The list is endless.

But if you really want to do your friends a favor, share the concept of pro-suming with them. If you want to give a gift that keeps on giving, tell your friends how *consuming takes money OUT* of their bank account, whereas *pro-suming adds money TO* their bank account.

Think of it this way. Which bank would you recommend to your friends? The bank that charged the cheapest rate for checking accounts in town? Or the bank that gave you money back every time you wrote a check, plus would give you a commission every time someone you referred to the bank wrote a check?

Okay, let me ask it this way. If a friend of yours banked at the second bank and did NOT tell you about it because he "didn't want to bother you," how would you feel? Would you be happy with your friend for not hassling you? Or would you be angry with your friend for not letting you in on the best deal in town?

The same goes for the opportunity of Referral Commerce. It's like banking at the Referral Commercial Bank. You write them a check for $100, they write you a check for $20. Same goes for anyone you refer to the bank, plus you get a commission on every check they write, plus a referral on the checks everyone in their referral organization writes.

If a Referral Commercial Bank opened in your community, wouldn't you want a friend to tell you about it? And wouldn't you want to tell all your friends and relatives about this amazing new bank that wrote checks to you when you wrote checks to them? *Of course you would — that's what friends are for!*

Would You Rather Grow Poor Slower?... Or Rich Faster?

Consumers beware! Superstores and deep discount websites may offer big discounts, but in the long run, it's not what you pay but what you get in return that counts. *And what could be better to get in return than the opportunity to own your own business and earn more money?*

We need to break out of the consumer mentality that tells us that cheaper is better. Cheaper isn't better. When we buy cheaper, we just get poor slower. *But when we buy smarter, we position ourselves — and our friends — to get rich faster.*

Now, I ask you, which would you prefer — to get poor slower? Or to get rich faster? It's a no-brainer!

If you're paying for products and services and aren't getting any money in return, ask yourself, "Why not?"

The answer could change your life.

9

E-FERRAL COMMERCE: PRO-SUMER POWER ON THE INTERNET

Everybody doing business directly —
to me that's the power of the Internet.
— Michael Dell
Founder & CEO of Dell Computer

From day one, Referral Commerce has welcomed technology with open arms.

Unlike traditional companies that avoid change at all costs, Referral Commerce has always invited innovation and change. Industry pioneers understood from the beginning that without technological advances, Referral Commerce would never reach its full potential.

The advent of affordable computers, for example, enabled referral-based companies to keep track of ever-changing and ever-expanding referral networks.

Cheap long distance rates allowed people to refer products and expand their businesses across continents and around the globe.

Innovative communication devices such as fax machines... cell phones... and audio and video machines made it easier and more cost effective for average people to build big, profitable referral organizations.

Each time an innovative, time-saving device hit the market, referral-based partners snapped it up and put it to use. As technology grew, so did the Referral Commerce industry.

The Internet Explodes onto the Scene

And then, seemingly out of nowhere, the most amazing technological breakthrough in history exploded onto the world scene — BOOM! THE INTERNET!

At first, traditional companies didn't know what to do with this thing called the Internet. It was so, well, unconventional. So loosely structured. So open. So massive. So unruly.

Traditional companies were besieged by hard-to-answer questions: How do we harness the Internet's speed and reach? How can the Internet make our business more efficient? And most of all, how do we keep the Internet from "cannibalizing" our bricks-and-mortar operations?

Forward-looking Referral Commerce companies, on the other hand, immediately recognized that *the explosion of the Internet wasn't something to be feared — it was something to be embraced*! If cell phones and fax machines could dramatically grow the Referral Commerce industry, just think what the Internet could do! The potential for referral-based companies to grow their business on the Internet was not just exciting — it was mind-boggling!

e-ferral Commerce: The Next Great Step in the e-volution of Referral Commerce

Burke Hedges, industry expert and author of three best-selling books about Referral Commerce, coined the term "e-ferral Commerce" to describe the marriage of Referral Commerce and e-commerce, and he made this bold prediction about the future of commerce on the Internet:

> *The Internet is all the rage right now. Everywhere we go we hear about e-commerce... e-banking... e-tailing... e-this and e-that. But when the cyberdust settles, the biggest winners in e-commerce will be off-line companies that successfully transition themselves to this new on-line medium called the Internet.*
>
> *Referral Commerce companies, with their bricks-and-mortar distribution systems already in place, are perfectly positioned to make the transition to clicks-and-mortar Internet sites. Referral Commerce has enjoyed explosive growth over the last 50 years, but that growth will pale in comparison to the future growth of e-ferral Commerce.*
>
> *When it's all said and done, deep-discount e-commerce start-ups that continue to operate in the red — such as Amazon.com — may make the front page news. But it will be the e-ferral Commerce companies and their pro-suming partners who make the profits.*

I agree with Hedges' assessment of Internet commerce. There will be a lot of shake-out on the Internet in the coming decade, just as there is in any new industry. The brilliant investor Warren Buffett likes to remind people that when the automobile industry was just gearing up in the first half of the 20th century, there were 3,000 different companies making automobiles in the U.S. Today there are only three major car manufacturers in the U.S. What happened to the 2,997 car companies that didn't make it? They were either bought out, or, when they couldn't turn a profit, they went out of business.

The same thing will happen on the Internet, only much faster! Companies will come and go at lightning speed. The promising ones will be bought out. The unprofitable ones will close their doors. It's Capitalism 101 — a few winners and lots of losers.

The Pro-sumer Advantage

I've taught marketing at the college level for nearly 20 years, but that doesn't mean I have a crystal ball that will allow me to predict which e-commerce companies will thrive and which ones will die. But I do know this — e-commerce companies will have to meet two big challenges head on in order to survive: One, they'll have to do something to keep their customers coming back; and two, they'll have to make a profit.

That's why e-ferral Commerce companies have such an advantage on the Internet — their pro-suming business affiliates have a built-in incentive to keep coming back. The more products a customer/affiliate buys, the deeper the discount they receive. And the more business they refer, the more referral fees they earn. *That's pro-sumer advantage number 1.*

Pro-sumer advantage number 2 is brand loyalty. Many referral-based companies offer one-of-a-kind products that can only be bought through referral partners. And brand loyalty is hard to break.

My parents, for example, have owned Buicks for 50 years. Are Buicks the cheapest cars on the market? No. Would my parents switch brands to save a thousand bucks? Not a chance! They're Buick people, and that's that!

Why Companies Spend Billions on Branding

Research shows that people buy brands because they have faith in the product and because it makes purchasing decisions a lot easier. When my parents are in the market for a new car, they drive down to the Buick dealership. They don't have to agonize over their decision. Or waste time test-driving other cars. Or do exhaustive research on the Internet. Or compare prices.

They just look over the new models in the showroom, choose the model and color they like best, sit down with the sales manager, and an hour later they drive off in a brand new Buick. It doesn't get any easier than that. Buying brands saves my parents time, reduces anxiety, and offers them comfort and assurance in a world filled with too many options.

That's why e-ferral Commerce companies have such an advantage on the Internet. Their customers keep coming back month after month because they love their one-of-a-kind products and services. In today's super-competitive, deep-discount-driven world, brand loyalty is key for companies that want to grow market share and profits.

Branding is why Nike paid Tiger Woods $40 million to wear the Nike swoosh on his hat and golf shirt when he first turned pro. Was Woods worth that kind of money just to promote the Nike logo? *No... in Nike's opinion, he was worth more!* Three years later Nike tore up Woods' $40 million contract and re-signed him for $100 million!

With e-ferral Commerce, Advertising Dollars Are Paid Out in Referral Fees

E-ferral Commerce companies have long understood the power of branding. But instead of paying one super-rich superstar athlete $100 million to advertise their brand, referral-based companies make that money available to their pro-suming partners in the form of referral fees. Which means that *instead of one superstar earning $100 million for his referral fee, Referral Commerce companies would spread that $100 million around by paying 1,000 average people $100,000 a year in referral fees for building their referral-based businesses!*

That's the power of e-ferral Commerce — each month thousands of satisfied customers can share millions of dollars in referral fees by leveraging the power and convenience of the Internet.

Now, I ask you... would you rather buy products on-line from a deep-discount-dot-com company that spends millions of dollars on clever commercials and celebrity endorsements in an effort to buy more customers? Or would you rather buy products on-line from an e-ferral Commerce company that spends zero on advertising and passes those savings on to its pro-suming partners in the form of referral fees?

To Pro-sume or Not to Pro-sume? — That Is the Question

Do you want to *consume your wealth* by buying on sale from someone else's e-commerce site, "They-Mart.com"? Or do you want to *create wealth* by buying on-line from your own e-commerce business, "My-Mart.com"?

Remember the line from the Mercedes commercial? *"It isn't always what you pay. It's what you get in return."* When you partner with a clicks-and-mortar Referral Commerce company, what you get in return is the opportunity to own your own e-commerce business and create wealth via the King Kong of Commerce, the Internet.

In the coming decade, thousands of people will be sharing millions of dollars in referral fees by way of e-ferral Commerce. Ask yourself, *"When I buy something on sale or on line, what am I getting in return?"* If you'd like to get the opportunity to own your own business and create wealth in return, then e-ferral Commerce could be the answer to your prayers.

One thing is for sure — whether you choose to get involved in the industry or not, e-ferral Commerce will explode in the coming decade, and thousands of average people will earn millions of dollars in referral fees by buying smarter, not cheaper, and teaching others to do the same.

Pro-suming Your Way to Financial Independence

The solution to get people out of debt and help them create lasting wealth for themselves and their families *isn't to stop consuming... but to start pro-suming*! It's just common sense.

Whenever I'm asked to talk to audiences about the key to wealth creation, I often begin with the joke about the brilliant young economist and the wise but uneducated farmer. The joke goes like this:

The city council of a small, midwestern town hired a world-famous economist to help straighten out the town's finances. The economist proceeded to talk for two hours using lots of fancy words and lofty theories. The townspeople listened politely, but they didn't understand a word the economist said.

At the conclusion of the speech, an old farmer stood up, turned to the audience, and condensed the economist's two-hour speech into one unforgettable sentence:

"Friends and neighbors, what this young man has been telling you is that if your OUT-GO exceeds your INCOME, then your UPKEEP will be your DOWNFALL."

The uneducated farmer understood that creating wealth is a matter of common sense rather than "book learning." And pro-suming is about as common-sensical as it gets — *buy smarter by buying from your own store and then teach others to do the same.*

Folks, ask yourself: "Would I like my income to exceed my outgo?"

"Would I like to make money while I spend money?"

"Would I like to build my own business and earn refer-ral fees by recommending quality products and services that people need and use on a daily basis?"

The secret to wealth isn't to stop consuming... but to start pro-suming! Millions of average people all over the world are pro-suming their way to financial freedom through e-ferral Commerce.

Which means you may want to ask yourself two more questions:

"Why not me?"

"Why not now?"

10

CLICK AND GROW RICH: THE E-FUTURE IS NOW!

*The Internet is not an add-on business.
It is a way to build an enormous new
business.*

— Sumner Redstone
CEO of Viacom

The DotComGuy — I suppose he was inevitable.
The movies *EdTV* and *The Truman Show* came
first, which isn't surprising given the fact that today reality imitates the movies, as opposed to the movies
imitating reality. So it was only a matter of time before a
"real" DotComGuy stepped into the spotlight.

On January 1, 2000, DotComGuy (formerly Mitch
Maddox, 26-year-old computer systems manager) entered

an empty house in Dallas carrying only a laptop computer and a handful of credit cards. DotComGuy plans to live exclusively on-line for one full year, during which time he will buy all of his necessities on the Internet, including food, furniture, and clothes.

DotComGuy can have visitors, but they aren't allowed to bring him any supplies or gifts, and he can venture no further away from his house than the backyard.

His sponsors hope to create awareness of their websites by broadcasting a 24-hour live video feed of DotComGuy's new on-line life. Dozens of digital cameras have been set up throughout the rented house.

"Our vision is that new on-line shoppers will go to our site to learn how to utilize e-commerce," said Maddox. Among his first on-line buys were shampoo, toilet paper, cleaning supplies, groceries, and carry-out food.

"We certainly don't recommend that people lock themselves away from the world," said Len Critcher, president of DotComGuy, Inc., "but we will prove that it can be done."

So, how does DotComGuy expect to make money to pay his e-commerce bills? His sponsors are paying him $24 a month, but the fee will double every month as an incentive to stay in the house. Doesn't sound like much, does it? But remember — DotComGuy's pay of $24 a month grows exponentially. Near the end of this chapter we'll do the math — and you'll see why the DotComGuy isn't so wacky after all....

It's a Wired, Wired World, After All

Like I said, it was inevitable that the Internet would give birth to a DotComGuy or Gal. Nowadays people will do almost anything to attract attention to themselves. But the story of DotComGuy teaches us two important lessons as we enter the 21st century.

Lesson one: *The Age of the Internet is no longer something that will happen in the future.* The Age of the Internet is here. Today. Right now. Sure, it will morph and merge and blend and grow in the coming decade. But make no mistake, the Internet is so powerful and so pervasive that today literally millions of people could work and live on-line without ever having to leave the comfort of their homes. To paraphrase Yogi Berra, "The future is nearer than it used to be." Truth is, the future is now.

Lesson two: *To a greater or lesser degree, we're all DotComGuys and Gals.* The world is wired, and each day thousands of new people sign up on the Internet. If you aren't on-line today, you will be tomorrow. Experts predict that one billion people worldwide will have Internet access by the first decade of the 21st century. That means that one out of every six people in the world will be networked to each other. The possibilities are endless.

Turning DotComGuys and Gals into Pro-sumers

It's fair to say DotComGuy will buy at least $20,000 worth of products and services during his year on-line. Now, let me ask you a question: What if DotComGuy spent that $20,000 as an *on-line pro-sumer, instead of an on-line consumer,* and then taught others to do the same? He'd not only be living on-line, *he'd be creating wealth on-line, wouldn't he?*

If DotComGuy were partnered with an e-ferral Commerce company, he could own his own business and be making money while he spent money! What a concept — *click and grow rich!* You see, that's the power of e-ferral Commerce — it's pro-suming on the Internet. Buying from yourself on-line can create wealth for you and your family, whereas buying on sale from a store or on-line from a deep discount e-commerce site reduces your net worth.

Robert Stuberg, author of *12 Wealth Secrets*, says the key to wealth is to reevaluate your spending habits. His common-sense advice sounds just like pro-suming in action:

> *You should really look at every purchase you make as an investment. Adding this leverage to your spending will do so much to increase your savings and returns that your wealth will accumulate faster than ever.*

Stuberg understands that spending money on investments produces income, while spending money on liabilities produces outgo. Pro-suming enables you to put Stuberg's advice into practice. When you partner with a Referral Commerce company, you have the opportunity to "look at every purchase as an investment." Instead of spending money on liabilities from K-Mart or Wal-Mart, Referral Commerce enables you to invest in your own store — "My-Mart."

A Million My-Mart.coms

Now, let's assume you see the wisdom of partnering with an on-line Referral Commerce company. When your referral-based company moves on-line, your Referral Commerce business evolves into an e-ferral Commerce business. If you think of your off-line referral-based business as My-Mart, then your on-line e-ferral business would become My-Mart.com. With My-Mart.com, you enjoy all of the advantages of pro-suming, coupled with all of the advantages of e-commerce.

Like DotComGuy, there are certain things you have to buy month in and month out in order to live. The first purchases DotComGuy made on the Internet would likely be the same ones you make every month — shampoo, toilet paper, cleaning supplies, nutritional supplements, and groceries.

But unlike DotComGuy, you'd be buying those products from yourself at My-Mart.com... and then teaching others to set up their own My-Mart.coms... and then helping them to teach others to set up their own My-Mart.coms... and so on.

By buying smarter on-line, and then teaching others to do the same, you could earn referral fees and create wealth for yourself while you help your friends and your friend's friends create wealth for themselves. *Click and grow rich, indeed*!

The Loser Gets the Same Prize as the Winner

On-line shopping offers two big advantages for consumers — convenience and lower prices. But it also comes with two big disadvantages — *convenience and lower prices*.

"Say what?" I thought you just said convenience and lower prices were advantages. And then you turn around and tell me they're disadvantages. Make up your mind....

You read it right the first time — *convenience and lower prices are BOTH an advantage and a disadvantage*. Let me explain.

The Internet is in its infancy. Before long the Internet will merge with your TV and your cell phone and every appliance in your home. In a few short years, you'll walk by your refrigerator and it will announce, "You need butter, eggs, and milk. Shall I order them for you?"

Before long you'll turn on the TV, and if you like the outfit that one of the actors is wearing, you'll be able to click on the actor and an on-screen box will appear indicating the brand name and price of the merchandise. Because your size, address, and credit card information will be stored in a digital data base, all you have to do is pick the color you prefer. The next day, the merchandise will be delivered to your door. Now that's convenience.

One problem. It's *too* convenient! The Internet makes

spending easier than ever before... and as the technology improves, buying will just get easier and easier and easier, which means your spending will go up and up and up.

Remember the lesson we learned from the Mercedes commercial: *It's not always what you pay. It's what you get in return.* If consumers can click on a TV character and buy a suit, what will they get in return? Only a liability that diminishes in value, correct? When consumers walk by the refrigerator and order eggs and butter and milk, what do they get in return? They get perishables that have zero value once they're consumed, correct?

Buyers beware! On-line consumers may think they're getting great prices and lots of convenience, but what are they getting in return? What they'll get is a smaller bank account. More liabilities. And fewer assets. Now do you understand what I mean when I say convenience and lower prices can be disadvantages?

The growth of e-commerce reminds me of a cartoon written and illustrated by Robb Armstrong, creator of a syndicated series called *Jump Start.* This particular cartoon is poking fun at the wildly popular TV game show, *Who Wants to Be a Millionaire?*

In the first panel, a husband and wife are watching a make-believe TV game show. The host announces, "Stay tuned for *Who Wants to Be Wildly in Debt?!*"

In the center panel the wife says, "It's a new reality-based game show...."

The final panel features this exchange:

Wife: *"The winner gets a charge card with an enormous credit limit at 26% interest..."*

Husband: *"I've heard of this show. The loser gets the same prize."*

The same goes for buying products off the Internet. The winners and losers of e-commerce get the same prize — convenience and lower prices. Which means e-commerce can either be a Godsend or a curse, depending on whether people choose to *spend money* by consuming or *make money* by pro-suming.

The Pro-sumer Advantage

Folks, if money seems to fly out of your pocket now, just wait a few years. Ever heard of the phrase, "cashless society"? Well, it's right around the corner, and it will make spending easier than ever before.

Did you ever stop to think why gamblers in Las Vegas have to convert their paper money to plastic chips? It's because, psychologically, a stack of poker chips worth $1,000 has a lot less perceived value to the gambler than a stack of $100 bills. It's a lot easier to toss a chip onto the roulette table than it is to peel off a $100 bill.

Same goes for credit and debit cards. They're plastic. Which means psychologically, they aren't real money. That's why it's a lot easier to buy merchandise on your charge card. Psychologically, your credit card purchases are "free" — that is, they're "free" until the credit card statement appears in the mail box. Reality check!

Here's my point. Because the Internet will make buying easier and easier in the years ahead, *it's more and more crucial that people position themselves to become pro-sumers, rather than consumers.* We're going to be buying more and more stuff on the Internet in the years ahead. That's a given. Since we're going to be spending money on the Internet anyway, doesn't it make sense to partner with an e-ferral Commerce company so that we can make money while we spend money?

Doesn't it make sense to create wealth by buying smarter on-line rather than cheaper on sale, and then teach others to do the same?

Doesn't it make sense to invest in our own business by buying products and services from My-Mart.com, rather than creating wealth for owners and shareholders of They-Mart.com?

What Does the "e" in e-ferral Commerce Stand For?

As we've discussed, e-ferral Commerce is the marriage of Referral Commerce and e-commerce. The "e" in e-commerce stands for *electronic*, as in the speed of light. But when you combine e-commerce with Referral Commerce, the "e" stands for a word that is just as powerful and dynamic as electronic. That word is *exponential*. And the exponential factor is what sets e-ferral Commerce apart.

To better understand the power of exponential growth, let's return to DotComGuy. Do you remember how he got paid? He'll get $24 the first month, and it will double every month he stays in the house. Now, excepting a few third-world countries, $24 a month isn't much of a wage. When it doubles to $48 the second month, and then $96 the third month, DotComGuy is still earning far below minimum wage.

But look what happens over time. By month seven, DotComGuy will earn $1,536 for that month's work. Month eight, he'll earn $3,072. By month nine, he's starting to earn some serious money — $6,144. Month ten, he'll earn $12,288. Month eleven, he'll earn $24,576. *And month twelve, he'll earn $49,152 — for one month's work!*

What you're seeing is the power of exponential growth at work. You see, exponential growth gets more and more powerful over time. The short-term gain for DotComGuy is small, just as it is in e-ferral Commerce. *But the long-term potential gain is huge!*

DotComGuy will be doing the same work in month twelve that he did in month one — *but he will be paid 2,000 times more money!* Why? Because of the Law of Compounding.

That's the power of exponential growth — small, con-

100

sistent efforts in the beginning yield small returns. But over time, those same small, consistent efforts can compound, yielding potentially huge, huge returns as your business grows exponentially, day after day, month after month, and year after year.

Just imagine receiving a check for $49,152 for one month's work. Sound impossible? Not at all. Thousands of people all over the world are receiving checks that size... and more!... by leveraging the power of Referral Commerce.

That's what can happen when people defer short-term gains in favor of a long-term investment. And that's what can happen when people build large referral-based organizations by buying smarter, not cheaper, and then teaching others to do the same.

That's why I say the "e" in e-ferral Commerce stands for two words, electronic and exponential. But thousands of average people worldwide are discovering that the "e" stands for a third word — *excitement*. Because EXCITEMENT is the emotion referral-based partners feel when they receive their monthly check for rebates and referral fees.

Electronic... exponential... and *excitement*. If you'd like to add those three words to your life, then you need to investigate e-ferral Commerce, an opportunity that many experts are calling "the opportunity of the New Millennium!"

CONCLUSION

DON'T DISCOUNT
YOUR DREAMS!

*We are the music-makers, and we are the
dreamers of dreams,... we are the movers
and shakers of the world forever, it seems.*
— Arthur O'Shaughnessy,
from *Ode*

The story I'm about to tell you is true. It contains a
powerful message that can transform your life
and the lives of those you care about the most.
Here's the story:

Years ago a minister and his wife were traveling through
rural Tennessee. They stopped at a restaurant for dinner.
A man walked into the restaurant, and all of the patrons
seemed to know him. He went from table to table greet-

ing everyone, and they were obviously delighted to receive his attention.

The man stopped by the minister's table, and upon discovering the minister's profession, the man sat down and shared his amazing story.

"When I was a little boy," the man began, "I grew up not far from this restaurant. My mother was unwed when I was born. In a small Tennessee town, that caused quite a bit of gossip and resentment. People treated my mother cruelly, ridiculing her and shutting her out of society.

"As a child, I received the same treatment. I was taunted and shunned at school. I had no friends. As a result, when I grew older, I kept to myself more and more.

"One day when I was almost 12, a new minister came to town. People said he was a gifted preacher... that he could deliver terrific sermons. They spoke so highly of him that I just had to go see him for myself.

"Week after week I would go to the church and listen to this wonderful preacher. However, I always made sure to leave before the end of the service. I could hear people whisper when I came in, and I knew they were thinking, 'What's a boy like that doing in church?' I didn't want them to have a chance to say it to my face.

"Then one week the sermon was so good, so enthralling, that I forgot to leave early. Suddenly, the service was over. And to my surprise and horror, the pastor came right over to my pew and spoke to me.

"'Who's son are you?' he asked.

"The congregation froze. The church was suddenly as quiet as a tomb. I was so embarrassed that all I could do was look down at my feet. I could barely breathe.

"The preacher immediately perceived that he'd made a blunder. Without a moment's hesitation, he smiled broadly, straightened his shoulders, and announced in a loud, even voice so that all in attendance could hear:

"'Oh, I recognize you. The resemblance is unmistakable. You're a child of God. He must be very proud of you!'"

The man's voice cracked slightly at the end of the story. But he took a deep breath and finished his visit with these words:

"That day changed my life. It gave me such confidence. In fact, I went on to become a pretty successful politician."

Then the man excused himself and made his way to the exit, slapping backs and shaking hands all the way.

When the waitress presented the check, the minister asked her if she knew the friendly man who just left.

"Why, yes. Everybody knows Ben Walter Hooper. He's the former Governor of Tennessee."

Isn't that a wonderful story? It shows the power of affirmation and positive thinking. Once Hooper changed his thinking, he changed his life. Instead of telling himself he was unworthy because he was illegitimate, he started telling himself he was just as good as the next person, because he was the child of God. That one simple but dramatic shift in thinking took an outcast to the governor's mansion. Amazing!

Change Your Thinking, Change Your Life

My friend, you, too, can change the direction of your life by changing your thinking. During the course of this book I've told you about an amazing opportunity called pro-sumerism with the hope that my message will change your thinking about the way you buy products and services.

My goal in writing this book was to persuade a majority of readers to change their thinking from consumer mentality to pro-sumer mentality. Hopefully, you're one of the readers who understands the power of pro-suming.

But in order to create the wealth you deserve and to live up to your full potential, you need to make another change in your thinking — a bigger change. *You need to change how you think about yourself,* just as a young Ben Walter Hooper changed the way he thought about himself.

You see, I used to think that people avoided change and ignored great opportunities because they were afraid of failure. And, yes, many people do avoid change for that reason.

But as I've gotten older and wiser, I've come to realize that *more people are afraid of success than are afraid of failure.* People who fear success avoid success, or, worse yet, they sabotage success because they don't think they're worthy of it.

We're Conditioned to Feel Unworthy

Like the child in the story, we're all conditioned to feel unworthy. We internalize the criticisms we hear. We buy into the limitations that people assign us. As a result, we all carry a stunted child inside of us, no matter how old we are. And, all too often, that inner child keeps reminding us over and over that we're not worthy.

We've been conditioned from birth to believe that we should place a ceiling on our ambitions because we're worthy of a little, but not a lot.

We've been conditioned to think that we're worthy to be employees, but not owners.

We've been conditioned to believe that we're worthy to earn a comfortable living, but not financial independence.

We've been conditioned to believe that we're worthy of being a follower, but not a leader.

We've been conditioned to believe that we're worthy of retiring at 65, but not at 45.

We've been conditioned to believe that we're worthy of taking a job, but not of seizing an opportunity.

We've been conditioned to believe that we're worthy of living little dreams, but not of living big dreams.

I say, "Nonsense!" *Don't discount your dreams!* Don't sell yourself short! You're worthy of success.... You're worthy of financial independence.... You're worthy of leading.... You're worthy of owning your own business....You're worthy of living big dreams. Do you know why? Here's why:

I recognize you. The resemblance is unmistakable. You're a child of God. He must be very proud of you.

You're Worthy of This Opportunity

Folks, don't procrastinate and sweep this opportunity under the rug because you don't think you're worthy of success. Don't ignore the message in this book because you don't think you're worthy of the benefits that e-ferral Commerce can offer you.

This opportunity is real. It's growing as big and as fast as the Internet. And thousands of average people who have changed their thinking are building global e-ferral businesses and earning substantial monthly referral fees for their efforts. For the first time in their lives, thousands of people are realizing that success and financial independence aren't reserved for others. Success is available to anyone who takes the time to buy smarter, not cheaper, and then teaches others to do the same.

Millions of open-minded people have changed their spending habits... and changed their thinking habits. As a result, they've become proud of their accomplishments... proud of owning their own business... proud of their new-found prosperity... and proud that they reached out and grabbed this opportunity.

Go ahead — make yourself proud. Reach for the brass ring. You *are* worthy. I challenge you to change your thinking by learning more about the opportunity of e-ferral Commerce. I challenge you to change your life by buying on-line from yourself through e-ferral Commerce, and then teaching others to do the same.

And always remember: No matter what happens in your life, you're a child of God.

He must be very proud of you!